▼ ▼

Empowering the Second-Language Classroom:

Putting the Parts Together

By Huberto Molina
with Ralph A. Hanson
& Donna F. Siegel

Empowering the Second-Language Classroom:
Putting the Parts Together

By Huberto Molina
with Ralph A. Hanson & Donna F. Siegel

Copyright 1997 by Huberto Molina

Published by
Caddo Gap Press
3145 Geary Boulevard, Suite 275
San Francisco, California 94118 U.S.A.

ISBN 1-880192-23-3

List Price: $19.95

Library of Congress Cataloging-in-Publication Data

Molina, Huberto, 1926-
   Empowering the second-language classroom : putting the parts
together / by Huberto Molina, with Ralph A. Hanson & Donna F.
Siegel.
      p.   cm.
   Includes bibliographical references.
   ISBN 1-880192-23-3 (alk. paper)
   1. Education, Bilingual--United States. 2. Second language
acquisition. 3. English language--Study and teaching--Foreign
speakers. 4. Children of immigrants--Education--United States.
I. Hanson, Ralph A. II. Siegel, Donna F. III. Title.
LC3731.M65 1997
370.117'5--dc21   97-14647
                                                        CIP

▼ ▼
Contents

Chapter 2

Early Reading Instruction, Non-English-Language Background,
and Schooling Achievement 45

Chapter 3

Confronting "Unalterable" Background Characteristics
of English-Language Learners 59

Chapter 4

Learning School Reference Concepts inthe Child's First Language:
A Guide for Parents as Teachers 67

Chapter 5

Instructional Decisions Based on Second-Language and Socio-Cultural Research 77

▼ ▼
Acknowledgments

To my colleagues Ralph E. Hanson and Donna F. Siegel, who have collaborated with me on various studies throughout the years. I would also like to thank Juan M. Aguilera, Elizabeth Aguilera, and Ken De Greene, the copy editors.

Special thanks to my wife Lillian for her continued interest and support in this absorbing project which deserves attention.

—*Huberto Molina*

About the Authors

Huberto Molina is an associate professor of elementary education at California State University, Northridge, and an instructor in cross-cultural language and academic development (CLAD) with the University of California Los Angeles Extension. He has previously taught grades K-12 with the Stockton and Acalanes School Districts and teacher education classes at the University of California Irvine. He has served as senior research associate at the Southwest Regional Laboratory for Educational Research and Development (SWRL) and is the principal author of the *English Language and Concepts Skills Program (K-8)*. He received his Ph.D. degree from the University of California Los Angeles.

Ralph A. Hanson is president of Hanson & Associates. His special areas of interest are testing and evaluation. He received his Ph.D. degree from the University of Chicago.

Donna F. Siegel is an assistant professor of education at the University of Science and Arts of Oklahoma. Her special areas of interest are teacher education and evaluation. She received her Ph.D. from the University of Tulsa.

Empowering the Second-Language Classroom

The Classroom Teacher Provides:
◆ Comprehensive Input
◆ Low Affective Filter

Classroom Supports:
◆ Bulletin Boards
◆ Learning Centers
◆ Picture Files
◆ Flannel Boards
◆ Approaches
◆ Assessment...

Putting the Parts Together

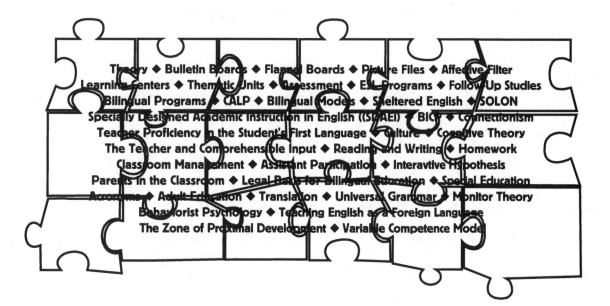

Theory ◆ Bulletin Boards ◆ Flannel Boards ◆ Picture Files ◆ Affective Filter
Learning Centers ◆ Thematic Units ◆ Assessment ◆ ESL Programs ◆ Follow-Up Studies
Bilingual Programs ◆ CALP ◆ Bilingual Models ◆ Sheltered English ◆ SOLON
Specially Designed Academic Instruction in English ((SDAEI) ◆ BICS ◆ Connectionism
Teacher Proficiency in the Student's First Language ◆ Culture ◆ Cognitive Theory
The Teacher and Comprehensible Input ◆ Reading and Writing ◆ Homework
Classroom Management ◆ Assistant Participation ◆ Interavtive Hypothesis
Parents in the Classroom ◆ Legal Basis for Bilingual Education ◆ Special Education
Acronyms ◆ Adult Education ◆ Translation ◆ Universal Grammar ◆ Monitor Theory
Behaviorist Psychology ◆ Teaching English as a Foreign Language
The Zone of Proximal Development ◆ Variable Competence Model

▼ ▼
Introduction

By Huberto Molina

Empowering the Second Language Classroom: Putting the Parts Together is written for those who are directly concerned with classrooms where a second language is being acquired: teachers, school administrators, teacher assistants, and parents. The text treats these three major topics:

♦ The *school context* in which a second language is acquired: bilingual and non bilingual models.

♦ A description and discussion of *approaches, methods, and techniques* used in those models.

♦ An emphasis on *teacher practices* which lead to second language acquisition and utilize resources readily available to all classrooms: bulletin boards; flannel boards; classroom walls, floors, ceilings, windows, and doors; learning centers; picture files; and the most important of all resources—students, parents, and the community.

These topics can be conceptualized in part as follows:

The Classroom:

The Teacher Provides:
- ♦ Comprehensive input
- ♦ Low affective filter
  - Motivation
  - Self-confidence
  - Low anxiety

The Classroom Supports:
- ♦ Bulletin boards
- ♦ Learning centers
- ♦ Picture files
- ♦ Flannel boards
- ♦ Approaches, etc.

Research studies referenced in the book support the recommended classroom practices. The interactions which underlie such instructional decisions are illustrated below. The various topics treated relate to the following framework:

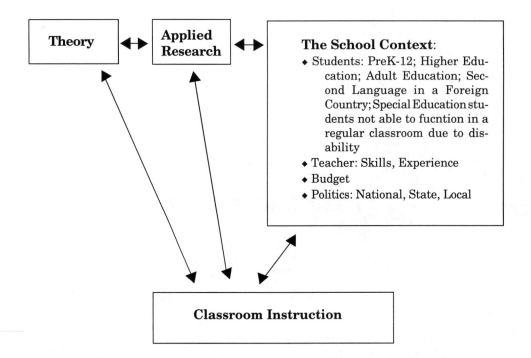

▼1▼
Ways to Empower
the Second-Language Classroom

By Huberto Molina

Overview

As I write this introduction, I am addressing the question: How can the classroom environment be incorporated into a rich language and subject matter experience for the student acquiring a second language? Although the classroom environment provides meaningful input from various sources, the critical player is the teacher who brings the parts together and provides meaning to those various parts.

The Classroom Context

In a sense, the classroom teacher is the artist. The theory, methods, and materials are the palette. Resources and approaches that a teacher can use in the important task of teaching a second language merit serious discussion. The topics presented in this chapter are discussed from the perspective of maximizing comprehensible input in an environment which serves as a low affective filter for instruction and learning. The need for comprehensible input in language instruction calls for a classroom that provides many opportunities for participation in activities which are understood by the student. Related to this need is the requirement for a low affective filter, a combination of classroom atmosphere and instruction that will reduce student stress. Students' energies are thus focused on rich language experiences in an unstressful classroom environment.

Among the programs, approaches, and techniques related to teaching a second language to be discussed are the following:

- ◆ Theory;
- ◆ Bulletin boards;
- ◆ Flannel boards;
- ◆ Picture file;
- ◆ Learning centers;

- Thematic units;
- Assessment;
- ESL and bilingual programs;
- Sheltered English (SEA)/Specially Designed Academic Instruction in English (SDAIE);
- The teacher proficiency in the student's native language;
- The teacher and comprehensible input;
- Reading and writing;
- Culture;
- Classroom management;
- Assistant participation;
- Parents in the classroom;
- Homework;
- Value of bilingualism.

Topics and approaches are presented here in such a manner as to apply broadly in the classroom. There has been a concerted effort to apply educational treatment independent of any particular text. Additionally, topics and approaches can be related to any second-language acquisition situation. English-as-a-Second-Language (ESL) is used as a case in point. ESL approaches can be used in teaching the learner a second language or to reinforce the home language. The classroom procedures and situations described are presented as examples. They should be modified by the teacher to fit grade level and language competency level. An attempt is made to suggest approaches and techniques utilizing inexpensive materials in common use in the classroom, materials that provide meaningful input relating to the reality of the classroom and to the outside world.

Theory and Second-Language Acquisition

Following are several of the key theories related to second-language acquisition, with some of the definiting characteristics of each theory and the names of key researchers responsible for development of the theories.

Universal Grammar

In the Universal Grammar model, language acquisition is viewed as an innate, species-specific, and governed by biological mechanisms. Though not a second-language acquisition theory, the Universal Grammar perspective has added insight to the second-language acquisition process.
Principal researcher: Noam Chomsky.

Behaviorist Psychology

In behaviorist psychology, language is viewed as a response system learned through operant conditioning. Behaviorist psychology is not a theory of language acquisition, but it is important as a tool for re-enforcement and appropriate practice of items already acquired, *e.g.*, classroom supports such as bulletin boards or learning centers.
Researcher: B.F. Skinner.

Connectionism

The model called Connectionism Parallel Distributed Processing assumes no innate endowment of language learning. Instead, learning consists of strengthening connections between and among simple processing units in complex neural networks.
Researchers: J. McClelland, D. Rumelhart, and M. Gasser.

Cognitive Theory

In cognitive theory, learning results from internal mental activity. Meaningful material can be integrated into existing cognitive structure.

Researchers: B. McLaughlin, J. Anderson, R. Shiffrin, W. Schneider, and D. Ausubel.

Monitor Theory

In Monitor Theory, the model proposed by Stephen Krashen consists of the following hypotheses:

1. Acquisition/learning;
2. Natural order;
3. Monitor;
4. Comprehensible input; and
5. Affective filter:
   Motivation, self-confidence, low anxiety.

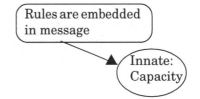

In Monitor Theory, the combination of comprehensible input and low affective filter cause language acquisition. The classroom and reading can provide comprehensible input.

Researcher: Stephen Krashen.

Critic of Monitor Theory: Barry McLaughlin. He argues that:

1. Focusing on form can aid in internalizing comprehensible input; and
2. Speech helps the speaker to test hypothesis.

Variable Competence Model

Negotiation plays a key role in learning a language, stressing the continuum between subconscious, automatic, and conscious analytic processes.

Researchers: E. Bialystock, R. Ellis, and E. Tarone.

Interactive Hypothesis

In the Interactive Hypothesis approach, input and learner production are considered important in promoting acquisition. Learners must interact and negotiate the type of input they receive.

Researcher: D. Long.

Source of Input and L1 Resources Model

The Source of Input and L1 Resources model considers the following:

1. Interaction between second language learners;
2. Sources of input;
3. Social setting;
4. Language acquisition second-language (L2) mechanisms operate less prominently in first language (L1) as compared to L2;
5. L2 learners tend to have well developed memory, pattern recognition, induction, categorization, generalization, reference capacities.

This model has relevance to adult L2 learners who may come to the classroom literate in their home language and who may speak several other languages.

Researcher: Lily Wong Fillmore.

The Zone of Proximal Development

According to the Zone of Proximal Development model, the learner brings two levels of development to the learning task:

1. What the learner can do;
2. What the learner will be able to do in the future.

The learner progresses through these levels using cooperative, meaningful interaction.

Researcher: L. Vygotsky.

Interaction of Theory, Research, School Context, and Classroom Practice

The Interaction of Theory, Research, School Context, and Classroom Practice model is in this text. It seeks to employ the school context as an input to classroom instruction, as demonstrated in the following chart:

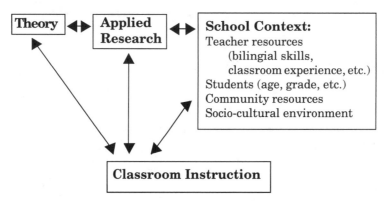

Second Language/Bilingual Education on the Elementary, Middle and High School Levels

The approaches and techniques described in this chapter, with appropriate age modifications, apply equally well to all three school levels—elementary, middle, and high school; however, it must be pointed out that instruction occurs in a different curriculum context at the various levels. In the elementary grades (K-6), students usually spend the entire day in one classroom under the supervision of one teacher. This allows maximum opportunity for continuity of instruction.

On the junior and senior high school levels, however, the school day is divided into periods (usually about an hour), each with a different subject matter teacher, only one of whom is usually responsible for providing English as a second-language instruction. In some schools a provision is made to present subject matter in a sheltered framework, *e.g.,* sheltered mathematics.

Another important factor influencing the curriculum offered at the different levels is that roughly two-thirds of the limited-English students are enrolled in the elementary grades. These greater numbers facilitate the grouping of limited-English students for diagnostic and instructional purposes. Another important factor is that the elementary school level provides the entry point for establishing a framework of instruction to follow in the school years ahead, while the middle and high schools draw students from various feeder schools, as well as transfers, all coming with quite diverse educational background experiences.

The Use of Bulletin Boards in the Classroom

Bulletin boards play a very important role in the instructional program; they are an important adjunct to the teacher's presentations. They go beyond brightening up a room environment, while that is important in its own right. Well-designed bulletin boards provide practice in the material being presented, and can expand the language and conceptual material presented by the teacher. Bulletin boards add excitement, utility, and recognition to skills that are being acquired.

As part of the teacher presentation, explicit reference should be made to bulletin boards in the context of the lesson being presented, so that learners can see the relationship between the teacher presentation and the display. Thus, learners become familiar with the bulletin board in terms of content, vocabulary, and conceptual framework before participating in the activity.

The bulletin board should present a meaningful experience to the learner. By being based on the language and conceptual repertoire that children are acquiring, and where possible by incorporating manipulatives, the bulletin board will allow learners to be able to put to use newly acquired skills in exciting and creative ways.

Let us examine some ways in which these objectives can be accomplished. In a health and nutrition unit, a bulletin board may display two paper plates which contain pictures of food pasted on the inside base of the plate. One plate may contain ice cream, cake, and candy, while the other plate may contain items that represent a balanced diet. The children themselves can participate in the process by preparing the plates, by pasting the illustrations cut from magazines. There is opportunity for the nutritional value of foods used by various cultures to be acknowledged, such as rice, beans, salsa, corn tortillas, pasta, etc. By changing the plates every few days, the experience can continue to be challenging and exciting.

Depending on the age of the learner and level of language acquisition, the complexity of the task can be adjusted. The response may be oral or written—in a one-word response. Written words, phrases, and sentences can also be used to describe why one plate contains a balanced diet or why it does not. Written answer cards can be provided by the teacher. These teacher-prepared cards could provide explanations, *e.g.*, "Yes, lettuce, tomatoes, and apples are good for you." "They are better choices than candy and doughnuts." "You chose the right answer."

A geography unit can be enriched by having a map of the world displayed on the bulletin board. The board may be entitled, "Where do you want to visit?" A student could tack one end of a piece of yarn to the bottom of the display and the other end to a country, *e.g.*, Japan. This bulletin board could very well be challenging all year-long by relating learning tasks to continents, countries, states, cities, rivers, and mountain ranges. This same bulletin board could be used to identify the countries of origin of the children in the class. This could be used as a spring board to discuss the uniqueness of other cultures and their contributions to the world and to the United Sttaes. In this way, geographical facts provide a basis for fostering respect for other cultures, even for those that may not be represented by students in the classroom.

As described above, many bulletin boards may be used for extended periods of time and can still be exciting and challenging by changing certain sections. Note that, as in the above example, bulletin boards can also be used as learning centers.

It is suggested that teachers photograph the bulletin boards they have used and keep the pictures on file for future reference, for it is easier to improve a board than to initiate one.

Bulletin Boards and Reading

On the kindergarten and first-grade level, a neat arrangement of items across the board can be used to illustrate left to right orientation. For older students, written words can be on cards which can be turned to illustrate the item. If the students read the item correctly, they can be rewarded by picking up a cut-out peanut to be used to "feed the monkey" illustrated on the bulletin board. This procedure can be varied to fit various holidays:

Christmas: A cut-out paper toy goes into Santa's bag.
Halloween: A cut-out Jack-o-Lantern is placed in front of a house.
Easter: A bunny rabbit receives a cut-out carrot.
Thanksgiving: A food item is added to a giant paper plate.

Words can be attached to a battery-powered board. When the correct connection is made between a word and a picture, a light goes on. Once you make up one board, you have the pattern to make a series of them. The boards can be made of cardboard or wood. In the higher grades, children can display their book reports or booklets that they have written. Students generally enjoy reading each other's work. On all levels, bulletin boards can be used effectively to encourage reading, an important source of comprehensible input to the second-language learner.

Form and Color in the Classroom

Bulletin boards can provide a sense of coordination, by using forms that repeat a pattern, such as rectangles of construction paper of the same color and size used to back the students' work. Colors repeated in the various boards can aid in the creation of a warm and coordinated classroom environment. A three-dimensional quality can be added by folding out paper, using cotton for cloud effects, and cellophane for water effects.

Recognition of Student Work

The bulletin board also provides an excellent opportunity to display the learners' class work, homework assignments, and other scholastic effort with due recognition. Opportunities should be designed so that all children in the classroom can display their efforts at one time or another.

Bulletin boards are valuable in displaying the effects of instruction to parents and the school administration. Displaying the various stages of development can be very effective in explaining the acquisition of skills through process. In the area of writing samples of students, initial scribbling, partial words, and complete words and phrases can make parents aware of normal developmental processes.

Flannel Board

A flannel board is structurally similar to a bulletin board. The board can be purchased or easily constructed by using plywood, cardboard, or by utilizing an existing blackboard as a backing covered by flannel. Cut-out flannel figures in various shapes and colors can be presented individually or superimposed. By placing the figures in a tray, students can pick up and place the items on the flannel board as they tell a story.

The flexibility that the flannel board provides makes it a valuable asset to any classroom situation where a changing scenario is present, *e.g.*, a thematic unit in which a topic covers many different items and unity and meaning have high priority. A flannel board is also very valuable in the reading process; first, by using cut-out figures to establish meaning, then by using strips from which students read. Flannel strips can also be used in writing activities.

A Picture File

A picture file is a very useful teaching device, and very inexpensive to create. The teacher, students, assistants, or parents can cut pictures from various sources, *e.g.*, magazines, newspapers, old calendars, etc. Picture files in two different sizes can be very useful. Large pictures can be mounted on posters measuring at least 8-1/2x11 inches for classroom use. Used manila folders make excellent backing for the large pictures. Index size cards can be used for small group or individual work. The two sizes can be used in conjunction with each other, *e.g.*, a student sees an item in a large context in the poster, then handles the smaller card supporting the verbal interaction. To sustain heavy usage the pictures should be laminated.

For ease of retrieval, the cards should be individually numbered with an accompanying index. The index should be based on the needs of the class. To illustrate, below is a partial index for the domain of *home*, with corresponding picture numbers:

Picture File Index

Domain:	Picture Number(s):
Home	
house	5, 37, 57
yard	7, 23
garage	2, 14
Other domains, etc.	

A picture should be crossed indexed under all relevant categories. For example, the picture of a yellow house would be indexed under *house* and *colors*.

Avoid Translation By Use of the Picture File

One use of the picture file is to avoid translation problems by going directly from the object or picture to the word or concept in the language being acquired, as exemplified in the following points:

1. In some classrooms students may be from different language groups, *e.g.*, speakers from Korea,

India, Israel, Mexico, etc. It is not expected that the teacher would be proficient in all these languages. Even if the teacher could communicate in these home languages, translation is not recommended for the reasons that follow.

2. Most vocabulary items do not correspond between languages on a one-to-one basis, *e.g.*, apple/*manzana*. *Manzana* for some Spanish speakers also means block, as in "The two houses are on the same block."

3. Even when learners speak the same language, some words may not be in use in the variety of the language spoken at home or in the language of the country of origin, *e.g.*, potato/*papa* or *patata*.

4. To go directly from the object or picture to the word is one operation. Going from the picture to one language, then to another language, involves two operation.

5. Another severe limitation is that once the learners are focused on the meaning of the word in the home language, they may not feel the immediate need for the word in English.

6. If a lesson is repeated in translation, this results in an inefficient use of class time.

7. Picture files help students acquire a second language by establishing meaning in the language being acquired and strengthening the learner's framework of the new language. For example, the teacher shows pictures of an apple and a pear. As the children identify the object, the teacher says: "That's right. This is an apple. This is a pear." Note that the students are hearing the use of *a* and *an* in a meaningful context. This meets a necessary requirement for acquisition by taking steps to add to current competency.

8. Picture files provide a framework for internalizing syntax. For example, the *box* is red. Mary has the *box*. The toy is *in the box*. The word *box* appears in different grammatical contexts.

9. Pictures, by focusing on meaning, facilitate use of simplification, paraphrasing, and gestures.

10. At times, even a native speaker will not be able to recall a translation of a word.

11. In addition to the above considerations, pictures add motivation and interest, and thus contribute to an acquisition-rich learning environment.

Using the File

A picture file has a great deal of utility, regardless of the students' stage of second-language acquisition. In advanced stages, the picture file can be used to make abstractions meaningful, *e.g.*, math, science concepts such as size, space relationships, etc.

Along with Total Physical Responses (TPR) activities, and manipulation of real items, the picture file finds extensive use during the "Silent Period." The "Silent Period" is a stage in which the students are internalizing the language, but are not yet ready to produce it orally.

There are many situations from various acquisition stages that illustrate use of the picture file. In one case, a puppet "Teddy" is used to initially carry out the task:

The teacher points to a car in a picture and says: "Point to the car, Teddy." Teddy points to the car. "Good, Teddy, you're smart." Following the procedure, the child then is asked to point to the car.

A picture file can present vocabulary items in various forms and in many different contexts. To illustrate, a stove can be pictured in a cabin, small house, big house, or restaurant. It can be an electric, wood, or gas stove. It can be a small inexpensive stove or a large expensive stove. By presenting different representations of an item, the students benefit in two ways: First, the students have numerous experiences with the item being learned and the bonding process of attaching meaning to form is strengthened. Additionally, by presenting the items in different forms, the learner can become aware of the variation of an item. In the case of a picture of a stove, multiple presentations help students become aware of the variety of items available within contemporary American culture. In a mathematics lesson, various configurations of a triangle can be seen and discussed. In both cases, the use of many different pictures adds clarity and interest to the lesson.

It takes time to build a picture file. One built by the class is more valuable than a commercially prepared one, because students have become a part of the process of attaching meaning to form. Have children bring to class pictures that hold special interest to them, *e.g.*, pets, farm animals, things they like to eat, etc. This is one way to personalize instruction and incorporate homework assignments, and also one that can involve parent participation.

There are many ways to use the picture file. The pictures can be used in a learning center, for example, where students can write stories based on the illustrations. "Story Starters" can be incorporated, where the first sentence is already written and the students add their own experiences to the story. Another variation is the "Picture Dictionary," in which a picture of an object appears on one side of a sheet or card, with the word on the reverse.

Learning Centers

Learning centers create a valuable opportunity to practice skills in a low-anxiety environment. Once the learner has acquired the required language skills necessary for the task, it becomes extremely important to provide as many opportunities as possible to practice those skills. The learning center can provide such opportunities to apply those skills. In designing the learning center, keep the following requirements in mind:

◆ The rules of conduct should be posted and modeled before the students participate. In the case of students learning a second language, modeling is very important, because the students are also learning what is appropriate behavior in a second culture.

◆ The design should allow for self-direction, independent work, and self-correction. The teacher should go over the learning center task with the class, so that students are very familiar with the activity before they participate individually. Self-correction mechanisms such as answer sheets, or question-answer segments that interlock when the response is correct, should be provided.

◆ The learning center should be designed to be used by all students regardless of ability.

◆ Topics should be relevant and interesting to the students.

◆ A title should appear on the center itself or on a bulletin board.

◆ Directions should be carefully explained before use and written on the learning center board.

◆ An answer box should be provided.

Learning centers offer great potential to the student by enriching and expanding familiar material covered in class. The self correcting mechanism supports a low-anxiety learning experience. In one way, learning centers offer an educational experience that may be even more valuable than the classroom lesson. Since there is opportunity to relate the learning center to real-life experience, the activity can make teaching relevant, *e.g.*, the word problem of the day requiring the use of mathematics skills taught in the lesson. The learning center can also be very effective in familiarizing students with various cultural holidays, *e.g.*, *Cinco de Mayo*, Fourth of July, etc. The center can be constructed in different sizes. Letter size centers can be easily stored. For the purpose of durability, lamination is suggested. Before laminating, all taping should be completed to ensure that the sections fold properly.

It is important to offer learning centers which foster critical thinking skills at an early age. To illustrate, as soon as students are able to read, they should start making distinctions between fact and opinion, for example:

> Today is Monday. (on reverse side, *fact*)
> It will rain next Monday. (on reverse side, *opinion*)

Learning centers can used in a variety of ways:

◆ They can be used to provide flexibility to accommodate the diversity of student performance, *e.g.*, those students who finish their work early can go to the center.

♦ By use of a schedule, a teacher can assign all students, at the same time, to different learning centers.

Following are a few sample topics that could be covered by use of a learning center:

♦ Geography.
♦ Holidays.
♦ Listening to recorded tapes.
♦ Recreational reading.
♦ Menus.
♦ Career education: professional careers, non-professional careers, college loans, etc.
♦ The financial world, *e.g.*, using the Stock Market, graphing a stock.
♦ Creative writing: stories, letter writing.
♦ Consumer education, *e.g.*, using a bank, grocery store, nutrition, etc.
♦ Using public institutions, *e.g.*, post office, department of motor vehicles, etc.
♦ Thinking and evaluation skills.
♦ Matching shapes, forms, etc.
♦ Sequencing events.

Thematic Units

Instruction presented under a central theme covering several days or extending into weeks is very appropriate to the second-language learner. Thematic units can tie known vocabulary and subject matter concepts to new material with meaningful continuity. The teacher has an opportunity to creatively weave the curriculum areas of language arts, social studies, mathematics, and science into a meaningful inter-relationship of learning activities. In the case of a second-language learner, it is critical to maintain meaning. A thematic approach makes it possible to extend the language and concepts, rather than treating each curriculum subject area separately. By using skills in different meaningful contexts, the acquired vocabulary and subject matter skills become increasingly relevant.

Assessment

Procedures used to identify and monitor progress of limited-English-speaking students are available in a variety of assessments, usually administered by the teacher or coordinator, a few of which are:

♦ A home-language survey completed by the students' parents. This information is used to identify the first language acquired at home.

♦ Assessment of language and literacy (reading and writing) in both home language and in English.

On the basis of the assessments and input from parents, children are placed at appropriate levels of instruction in both first- and second-language instructional sequences. The chart on the next page presents a sample of assessments in use in the entry/exit process in a bilingual program. The section at the bottom of the chart provides an index to the sequence of presentation of formal and informal assessments.

Assessment of Oral Skills

Students eligible for English-as-a-Second-Language instruction are typically placed according to how they communicate orally in the language. There is an increasing concern to use effective assessment instruments, requiring minimal training in their use by the classroom teacher. The teacher observes the students' language performance in the classroom and in a more structured setting using posters and pictures to engage in the assessment. Various settings in which students interact with teachers and with other students should be used in the assessment, *e.g.*, classroom, in the playground, talking with peers.

LEP Entry/Exit Assessment Process
Sample: English/Spanish

1

All parents fill out a **Home Language Survey** when the child enters the school.
This survey identifies students who may be limited English proficient (LEP).

 2

The **Language Assessment Survey (LAS)** identifies the proficiency in L1 and L2.
Students identified as Non- or LTD- (limited) proficient in L2 are placed in a full (language arts and content in L1 + ESL) or modified (language arts and math in L1, content in sheltered English + ESL), *or* in an ELDP (English Language Development Program, sheltered English + ESL) *if* parent requests English-only instruction.

 3

LEP students are periodically assessed in the L1 and L2 to monitor progress.
L1—(varies) Aprenda, CTBS-Español, PUENTE, SABE—assesses content and skills. L2—**SOLOM** (Student Oral Language and Observation Matrix)—assesses oral L2 development only. L1 & L2—Teacher-made tests, assessment of individual skills, progress matrix, other.

 4

Students must meet criteria to add transitional English language arts and content instruction.
Full/Modified—Reading and writing in L1 (usually at 2.2 grade level) + ESL (usually SOLOM level IV)— pass **CARE** (Spanish). Criteria assumes that threshold level is adequate to foster an additive bilingual process. ELDP—ESL and Reading Readiness

 5

Transitional Language Arts and Content Instruction (Full/Modified) *or* Sheltered Language Arts and Content Instruction (ELDP)

 6

Mainstream Language Arts and Content Instruction
Redesignation—RFEP (Redesignated Fluent English Proficient)

Formal Assessment			Informal Assessment		
Item	Language	Refer to...	Item	Language	Refer to...
(pre) LAS	L1	Box 2	Home Survey		
Aprenda	L1	Box 3	Survey	L1	Box 1
SABE	L1	Box 3	SOLOM	L2	Box 3
CARE	L1, L2	Box 4	Teacher-Made	L1, L2	Box 3
CTBS	L1 and/or L2	Box 3	or Skills Matrix		
Teacher-made	L1, L2	Box 3			

The commonly assessed areas are:

- Comprehension;
- Fluency;
- Vocabulary;
- Pronunciation;
- Language structure.

An example of this type of assessment is presented in the chart on the next page. Ratings typically are based on a one-to-five continumum in the categories shown on the chart, with 1 equated to extremely-limited-proficiency and 5 equated to approximating native language performance suitable for mainstream classroom participation. Explicit explanation should be provided to aid in the rating process. There is an attempt, generally, to assess natural use of language; however, in some assessments the students' proficiency is assessed by non-communicative use of language structure, *e.g.*, repeating isolated utterances, recognizing two words as the same or different, etc. The important outcome of the assessment should be that the results help provide appropriate instruction based on the students' level of readiness.

During the instructional program, students are then re-assessed in the five categories depicted on the chart. At the stage when the appropriate level is reached, usually overall ratings of 4 or 5, the students enter a transitional language arts program in the form of sheltered English, where they can increase English language skills while acquiring cognitive academic proficiency. The natural progression is from the least language-dependent courses—-mathematics and science—to social studies, which is linguistically more abstract. Reading and writing skills are commonly assessed using holistic approaches, calling again for ratings of over-all performance.

Teachers should be encouraged to develop rater reliability. This skill can be accomplished by two or more teachers comparing their ratings of student performance and aiming for high agreement, at a level of 80 to 90 percent.

In some classes a portfolio is used as the basis of assessment. The portfolio contains an organized collection of student work. It may contain, for example:

- Selected written assignments;
- Observations;
- Assessment and test scores.

Portfolios can be very effective in assessing students' progress and achievement over a time period and in teacher-pupil, teacher-parent, and parent-pupil discussions. Assessment is important in the classroom, but only if appropriate instruction follows. A low assessment score by itself merely states that a problem exists.

ESL and Bilingual Programs

In two of the major bilingual program models—the Maintenance Bilingual Program and the Two-Way Program—first-language skills are maintained and fostered during the instructional program. It may appear that native-language instruction is competing with time spent on English-language instruction; however, there is research to support the claim that English and other related cognitive skills are acquired faster and at no expense to English when a firm foundation of the first language is established.

It takes time to acquire a second language: approximately two to three years to function using basic interpersonal communications skills, which enable the learner to communicate in a minimal language environment. It takes five to seven years to acquire cognitive, academic language proficiency to be able to participate in mainstream second-language instruction.

English-as-a-Second-Language (ESL) is an integral part of the three major program models used in bilingual education in the United States. Those three models are:

- **Transitional Bilingual Program Model**: The goal is for the student to learn English with no attempt to strengthen the child's first language.

SOLOM Teacher Observation
Student Oral Language Observation Matrix

Student's Name: _____

Language Related:_____ Grade: _____   Date(s)

School:_____ Teacher:_____ Total Score(s)

Key word:	severe 1	difficulty 2	frequently 3	ocasional 4	approximate native speaker 5	Score
A Comprehension	Cannot understand even simple conversation.	Has great diffi-culty following everyday social conversation even when spoken slowly with repetition.	Understands most of what is said at slower-than-normal speed with repeti-tions.	Understands nearly every-thing at normal speed, although occasional rep-etition may be necessary.	Understands everyday con-versation and normal class-room discussion without diffi-culty.	
B Fluency	Speech is so halting and fragmentary that conver-sation is vir-tually impos-sible.	Usually hesi-tant; often forced into si-lence by lan-guage limita-tions.	Everyday con-versation and classroom dis-cussion fre-quently dis-rupted by the student's search for the correct manner of expression.	Everyday conver-sation and class-room discussion generally fluent, with occasional lapses while the student searches for the correct manner of expres-sion.	Everyday con-versation and classroom dis-cussion fluent and effortless approximating that of a native speaker.	
C. Vocab-ulary	Vocabulary limitations so extreme that conver-sation is vir-tually impos-sible.	Difficult to understand due to misuse of words and very limited vocabulary.	Frequently uses the wrong words; conver-sation some-what limited because of inad-equate vocabu-lary.	Occasionally uses inappro-priate terms and/or must rephrase ideas due to limited vocabulary.	Use of vocabu-lary and idi-oms approxi-mate that of a native speaker.	
D. Pronun-ciation	Pronuncia-tion prob-lems are so severe that speech is virtually unintelli-gible.	Difficult to un-derstand be-cause of pro-nunciation problems; must frequently re-peat in order to be understood.	Pronunciation problems neces-sitate concentra-tion on the part of the listener and occasionally lead to misun-derstanding.	Always intelli-gible, though one is conscious of a definite accent and occasional inappropriate intonation pat-tern.	Pronunciation and intonation approximate that of a na-tive speaker.	
E. Gram-mar	Errors in grammar and word order so se-vere that speech is virtually un-intelligible.	Difficult to un-derstand due to errors in gram-mar and word order; must of-ten rephrase and/or restrict speech to basic patterns.	Frequent errors in grammar and word order occa-sionally obscure meaning.	Occasional er-rors in grammar and/or word or-der do not ob-scure meaning.	Grammar and word order approximate that of a na-tive speaker.	
NA Category	Preproduc-tion	Early production I	Early Production II	Speech emergence	Immediate fluency	

♦ **Maintenance Bilingual Program Model**: The goal is to develop the child's proficiency in both languages.

♦ **Two-Way Enrichment Bilingual Model**: The goal is for speakers of the minority language to acquire English and for mainstream speakers to acquire the minority language.

In the following diagram is a summary of program types and brief descriptions is provided.

Programs and Approaches Used in Second-Language Instruction

Bilingual Programs				Non-Bilingual Programs	
Maintenance*	Two-Way Enrichment	Transitional	Immersion (Canadian Model)	L2 Only (English)	Submersion "Sink or Swim"
Minority students learn in L1 while acquiring English.	Language minority students acquire English. Language dominant students acquire minority language.	Minimal attention is provided for L1 as transition is made to English.	Langage dominant students acquire minority language.	◆ Pull-out (ESL) ◆ English Language Development (ELD). *Subject matter is learned while acquiring English language skills. Usually used on parent request that children not be enrolled in a bilingual program or where no bilingual program is available*	This approach is outlawed.

Characteristics

Minority language students acquire English at no expense to L1.	Advantage: both groups gain competency in two languages. Model provides for interaction between dominant and minority language speakers.	In Early Exit, the second language is acquired at the expense of the first language.	Second language is acquired at NO expense to first language. Model does not provide for interaction between minority and language dominant language speakers.	By limiting instruction to L2, L1 is not acknowledged as a national resource, as an individual asset, nor as an efficient way to learn subject matter in English through transfer.	Bilingual Education Act of 1968 outlawed this practice.

A modified bilingual program is used where there is a shortage of qualified staff to teach various language groups.

The following approaches can be used with the above program models: Sheltered English Approach (SEA), Cooperative Learning, Natural Approach (NA), Total Physical Response (TPR), and Learning Experience Approach (LEA).

Another bilingual program model in use on a limited basis in this country is the Immersion Bilingual Education model. Initially it began in Canada, where English-speaking children learned French from the first year in school. Immersion Bilingual Education has been used in Culver City, California, where English-speaking children learn Spanish. In the Two-Way Enrichment Immersion Programs, English-speaking students learn the minority language and non-English speakers learn English.

There are programs in use in the United States in which the only provision for bilingual students is an ESL-Only Program, which is usually a "pull-out" program. Structured Immersion follows this format. On the high school level a class period in the school day is provided for this purpose. In some high school programs sheltered instruction is provided in the subject matter area.

No matter which program is used, teachers should acknowledge the importance of the students' first language. It provides:

1. The connection to parents, family, and community.
2. A marketable asset to the child and to a global society.
3. A conceptual base which can easily be transferred to English-language literacy skills.

Sheltered English (SEA)/
Special Designed Academic Instruction in English (SDAIE)

Both of the terms, Sheltered English (SEA) and Special Designed Academic Instruction in English (SDAIE), describe academic instruction in English. The latter term better describes the instruction that is focused on academic instruction rather than on language development.

SDAIE qualifies to be called an approach to language instruction and acquisition because it is based on certain key *assumptions* that underlie the instruction.

Those SDAIE assumptions are:

1. SDAIE is concerned with the teaching of grade level subject matter in English specifically designed for limited-English-proficient (LEP) students.

2. SDAIE is designed for LEP students who possess basic literacy skills in the primary language, which provide a strong foundation to support rapid English-language development. Thus it is a key component in a bilingual program.

3. SDAIE is most appropriate for students who have reached a Speech Emergence Stage of proficiency in English (comprehension, speaking, reading, and writing). On an oral proficiency level, this corresponds generally to a three/four Solomon level, occurring usually in the third or fourth grade for those students who enter first grade speaking a home language other than English. SDAIE is especially significant at the third and fourth grade levels, for it is in these grades that language used in the classroom begins dealing with abstract, academic constructs.

4. SDAIE is not designed as a remedial program, nor a program for slow learners. It is designed to facilitate mastery in content areas while adding to English-language skills.

To support the above assumptions the following *strategies* are typically used in SDAIE programs:

1. Simplify the input:
   ◆ slower rate of speech;
   ◆ clear enunciation;
   ◆ controlled vocabulary;
   ◆ controlled sentence length;
   ◆ use of cognates;
   ◆ limited use of idiomatic expressions;
   ◆ use and explain where idioms are necessary to the understanding of content;
   ◆ definition of words with double meaning;
   ◆ mini-lectures;
   ◆ if lecture is necessary, present information in simplified, shorter lecture forms.

2. Check frequently for understanding in teaching concepts:
   ◆ check for comprehension;
   ◆ elicit requests for clarification;
   ◆ repeat information;
   ◆ paraphrase statements of information;
   ◆ expand statements of information;
   ◆ pose a variety of questions;
   ◆ pose questions of different levels;
   ◆ facilitate teacher-to-student and student-to-student interaction in summarizing;
   ◆ recap main topics and key vocabulary in a variety of ways.

3. Use contextual cues:
   - gestures;
   - facial expressions;
   - dramatization of meaning; pantomime, role playing, readers theater;
   - props;
   - visuals: graphs, study prints, photographs, slides, overhead projections, diagrams, maps, videotapes;
   - realia: artifacts, models;
   - bulletin boards;
   - word and topic clusters;
   - word banks;
   - tape recordings by native English speakers.

4. Design appropriate lessons:
   - consider students fluency level;
   - emphasize key vocabulary;
   - extend anticipatory set;
   - check for pacing;
   - include cooperative learning group techniques;
   - reading activities preceded by listening and speaking activities;
   - writing activities preceded by listening and speaking activities, hands-on experiences, brainstorming, word clusters, or mapping.

5. Focus on subject matter content:
   - identify key topics;
   - organize key topics around and identifiable objective;
   - choose topics appropriate to grade level.

(6). Keep lessons student-centered:
   - check for student attention;
   - employ a variety of grouping strategies;
   - provide manipulatives;
   - plan hands-on activities;
   - use many learning modalities: kinesthetic, auditory, oral, visual.

SDAIE Approach/SDAIE Strategies

The SDAIE approach described above is, as indicated, based on certain key assumptions; however, SDAIE strategies can be used at any grade level, ranging from kindergarten through high school and beyond. For that reason many of the strategies listed above are described in this text as independent topics for consideration.

Language and Content Items in Sheltered English/SDAIE

In preparation of SDAIE instruction, the academic content and language items are identified by analyzing the existing curriculum. This implies that once the items are identified, built-in assessment systems will be used to assure that learning has taken place and to determine when additional instruction is needed. A built-in assessment system should include a placement assessment, unit assessments, and an end-of-program assessment. The end-of-program assessment should include a provision for more learning opportunities, to review those items which have been covered in instruction, but have not yet been mastered.

After exiting from SDAIE to regular-English instruction, to assure that students have mastered the necessary skills to succeed in mainstream classes, a follow-up assessment should be administered during the subsequent school year. Teachers can rate pupils in terms of performance in English with classroom peers. Descriptive ratings can be specifically referenced to the following skill and achievement areas: reading, oral language development, writing, mathematics/science, and social studies. Teachers can rate student performances in terms of four ordered categories:

- Cannot do tasks.
- Experiences difficulty.
- Performs adequately.
- Excellent performance.

Following is a sample assessment sheet that can be used for rating an individual student. Scores can then be grouped.

Sample Assessment Sheet

Task	1 Cannot do Task	2 Experiences Difficulty	3 Performs Adequately	4 Excellent Performance
Reading: Interprets written symbols as meaningful communication.	❑	❑	❑	❑
Reading: Reads orally with fluent standard English, pronunciation and intonation.	❑	❑	❑	❑
Oral Language Development: Has sufficient control of language to ask and answer questions in class.	❑	❑	❑	❑
Oral Language Development: Has sufficient control of language to function in the classroom.	❑	❑	❑	❑
Writing Skills: Competency in writing skills.	❑	❑	❑	❑
Math/Science: Sufficient proficiency in using Math/Science concepts, *e.g.*, numbers, numerals, numeration, including adding and subtracting.	❑	❑	❑	❑
Math/Science: Identifies and names space relationships, comparisons, *e.g.*, above, under, big/bigger/biggest.	❑	❑	❑	❑
Math/Science: Identifies and names set concepts and basic geometric figures, e.g., members of a set, number of a set, circle, square.	❑	❑	❑	❑
Social Studies: Sufficient language proficiency to deal effectively with health and safety requirements at school.	❑	❑	❑	❑

By examining the rating results of the group, a basis can be initiated for assessing the effectiveness of the SDAIE experiences. Individual rating scores can be paired with attendance records to explain to parents the importance of school attendance. Other assessments, such as portfolios, can be used that more specifically identify subject matter areas in which students may have received sufficient or insufficient preparation for mainstream instruction.

Getting Ready For Assessment

It is important for ESL students to acquire the necessary test-taking skills. As stated previously, some assessment is performed by observation. In preparation for formal test-taking, it is important to prepare students for the task. The following activities are suggested:

- Fun activities using a learning center where children carry out test-taking task such as matching shapes, sequencing events (seed, seedling, tree), sequencing patterns (color each third item).

- Filling in a bubble like those that appear on a test form. For older students, reviewing for a test and using cooperative learning techniques can be very beneficial just prior to testing. The verbal interaction negotiation and over-learning that may be involved can be used to an advantage.

The Natural Approach (NA)

The Natural Approach is based on the following primary assumptions:

1. The Natural Approach is communicative-based with acquisition as a goal.

2. Second language is acquired in a manner similar to native-language acquisition, in contrast to learning the rules of the language.

3. Students need to receive comprehensible input in a rich acquisition, low affective filter environment.

4. The Natural Approach is mainly concerned with basic interpersonal communication skills (BICS).

5. Language is acquired in four natural sequential stages:
   ◆ Preproduction: Speech emerges in natural stages. This is followed by a transition Period, when the primary emphasis is still on listening comprehension through recognition of new lexical items.
   ◆ Early Production: Activities are designed to motivate students to begin language production.
   ◆ Speech emergence: Activities are designed to promote language expression.
   ◆ Intermediate Fluency: Activities are designed to attain mainstream performance levels

The primary techniques of the Natural Approach are:

   ◆ Concentrate on comprehension;
   ◆ Use SDAIE techniques;
   ◆ Use low anxiety situations;
   ◆ Avoid overt correction of forms;
   ◆ Do not force production before student is ready;
   ◆ Focus on interpersonal communication.

The Natural Approach has four main stages:

Stage 1: Concentrate on comprehension, use TPR (commands): body parts, classroom objects, people, naming people/ objects, nodding, body movement: walk/point/hop. Transition: Yes/no, here/there, extend aural vocabulary, "Who has the ____/picture of ____?"

Stage 2: Early Production: One/two word responses using above techniques, either/or questions, lists, short phrases, complete sentences, simple sentences.

Stage 3: Speech Emergence Stage: Long phrases, compels sentences, extensive vocabulary, correctness level improves, open dialog, skits, extended discourse, narrative, language experience activities.

Stage 4: Intermediate Fluency, Fluent, but lacking in CALP.

The following guide can be used to correlate SOLOM diagnostic scores to the above four levels of instruction:

1. Divide Early Production into two levels:
   Early Production I and Early Production II.

2.
Natural Approach Category	SOLOM Level
Preproduction	1
Early Production I	2
Early Production II	3
Speech Emergence	4
Intermediate Fluency	5

The Teacher's Proficiency in the Student's Native Language

The primary responsibility of the ESL teacher is to provide mean-ingful second-language input to students acquiring the language. Some program models allow more flexible use of teachers and accommodate team teaching. In many such cases, native speakers teach in the home language and in the second language being acquired. Such is the case in the Two-Way Enrichment Bilingual Program Model. This is the best model for two reasons. All children in the school benefit by acquiring a second language. Additionally, students receive instruction from a speaker with native-language capability.

In the Transitional Bilingual Program and Maintenance Bilingual Program models, it is assumed that the bilingual teacher is proficient in both languages.

In maintenance Bilingual Programs, specifically, it is important to establish a strong base in the first language and concepts, for these skills are the basis for learning the second language. Once learned, these skills easily transfer to English. With regard to use of Spanish, as an example, careful attention should be directed to the standard form of the language, for the following reasons:

1. Spanish-speaking students are now in our classrooms from many different parts of the Spanish-speaking world. Standard Spanish provides the base form.

2. Most commercial and academic environments are conducted using the standard form of the language.

3. Tests that students normally take to demonstrate threshold proficiency in the first language are written in standard Spanish.

These tests are used as criteria by which a student exits toward the mainstream English-language curriculum. The teacher should acknowledge and accept all forms of Spanish that students bring to the classroom, *e.g.* dialectical variants, "Spanglish," etc. They are all legitimate forms of communication. However, the teacher has the responsibility to provide the model and instruction of Standard Spanish for the reasons provided above. Students should be encouraged to prize their home dialects but, at the same time, add the standard form to their repertoire.

If a student uses a non-standard form, the communication should be acknowledged as correct, but the teacher should model the standard form.

In an ESL-Only program, the teacher should be a bilingual. If the ESL students in the class are from one major language, then there is a strong possibility that the teacher will be bilingual or have a bilingual assistant. If the class consists of various language groups, for very practical reasons the teacher will probably not speak the native language of each child. In this case, to maintain meaning all the techniques discussed in this chapter will have to be used to the greatest extent possible.

The Teacher and Comprehensible Input

How can the teacher maximize comprehensible input? Following are language areas, each with specific recommendations to assist teachers in such efforts:

Phonology
- Speak in a voice loud enough so that all can hear. This usually demands that the teacher speak louder than usual.
- Use clear articulation.
- Slow speech, but maintain natural intonation.

Words
- Enunciate the words carefully to enable students to be aware of units that make up words, *e.g.*, book/books.
- Choose high frequency cover words, *e.g.*, *tree* covers *pine*, *oak*, *laurel*, etc.

Sentence Structure
- Simplify syntax.
- Use short sentences.

Meaning

Teach a little beyond current competency and still maintain meaning by:
- Use real objects.
- Pictures.
- Act out meaning, use puppets, make use of role playing, etc.
- Use items that children can manipulate.
- Explain using different words.
- Use gestures.
- Encourage children to ask questions by gesture, by raising hand, and later by use of structures such as *who, what, where, when, why,* and **how**.
- Give students ample time to react.
- We communicate in different ways, by use of language, by use of language in conjunction with non-linguistic ways, and by non-linguistic ways alone.

Current Competency

Use bulletin boards and learning centers to practice current   competency in different contexts.

Non-Linguistic Communication
- Use of our hand to indicate STOP.
- Throwing up our arms to indicate surprise.
- Placing a finger over our lips to indicate silence.
- Grimaces indicating happiness, anger, fear.

Combine Non-Linguistic with Linguistic
- Speaking as we point
- Use of our hands to elaborate

In the early stages and types of language acquisition, one person uses language and the person acquiring the language uses non-linguistic means to communicate. This is the case when Total Physical Response (TPR) Approach is used, for example:

Teacher: Point to the book
Student: Points to the book

The role played by non-linguistic forms of communication provides us with a good reason why students should have a clear view of the teacher during the communication process. Pictures from the picture file can also be used to depict these important forms of meaningful communication.

Encourage students to interact and negotiate meaning with each other. In the empowered classroom, meaningful output produced by a student becomes comprehensible input to the listener.

Students, pre-kindergarten and on, will naturally interact with each other or talk to themselves as they participate in their learning activities. As long as conversations do not interfere with other classroom activities, this type of language production activity should be considered acceptable and valuable for language-acquisition purposes, such as talking to friends about their work as they carry out the assignment.

The teacher, teacher aides, and parent assistants can be very helpful in maximizing comprehensible input and meaningful output by encouraging:

- Discussion which promotes interaction between members of a group, *e.g.,* talking informally about the learning activity.

- Negotiation for meaning, *e.g.,* asking for further explanations, disagreeing with someone, asking questions, expressing an opinion, praising, etc.

The above forms of communication, expressed in a socially acceptable manner, are important in the empowerment of a classroom. Their use is an asset in the school environment and in real life. The following modeling techniques are suggested:

- Use a puppet to model acceptable behavior, *e.g.,* "Very good, Teddy." "You listened carefully and you did not interrupt while Mary was speaking."

♦ If a student continues to be disruptive, have a designated place where the child is asked to sit away from the class to think about the behavior. When the child is "ready," the student rejoins the class.

♦ As a continuing routine throughout the year, a student sits in front of the group and class members compliment or praise the student, *e.g.*, "Billy has a nice shirt, always listens carefully, always put his things away, etc." Teddy, the puppet, may also want to praise Billy.

These social skills can be used in formal group instruction, such as in cooperative learning.

Lesson Planning

To assure the most effective instruction possible in language acquisition programs and related classes, the teacher's lesson plan should include the following seven steps:

1. The objective: An overall and specific objective.

2. An introduction/anticipatory set:
   ♦ Identify key topics;
   ♦ Display and describe materials one at a time to be used in the lesson;
   ♦ Encourage discussion about items.

3. Directed lesson:
   ♦ Teacher presents lesson;
   ♦ Teacher models.
4. Guided Instruction:
   ♦ The teacher continues modeling and guides students through process.

5. Independent Practice:
   ♦ The teacher checks for understanding on the concepts;
   ♦ The teacher gives directions for the independent work;
   ♦ Students carry out activity.

6. Alternate and Supplementary Activities:
   ♦ Students can carry out additional activities provided by the teacher

7. Evaluation/Summary/Closure:
   ♦ Observe student work during Independent Practice;
   ♦ Journal writing;
   ♦ Use other forms of individual assessment.

In addition, the lesson plan should specify:
   1. All materials and equipment used in the lesson.
   2. Model at all levels: language usage, procedures, etc.
   3. Check for comprehension at all levels:
      ♦ by use of TPR techniques, *e.g.*,., students point;
      ♦ by student interaction;
      ♦ by asking questions asked by students and teacher.
   4. Indicate cognitive level by use of Bloom's taxonomy.

On the following page is a sample lesson plan format.

ESL Seven-Step Lesson Plan

Teacher_____

Date_____

Levels of Taxonomy Emphasized
____1. Knowledge
____2. Comprehension
____3. Application
____4. Analysis
____5. Synthesis
____6. Evaluation

Materials: puppet
              picture file
              drawing materials: paper, crayons

Equipment:

Procedures to be included in all 7 steps:
   ◆ Check for comprehension: Use TPR, ask questions, etc.
   ◆ Model at all levels: Model by repeating procedures and use key vocabulary in a variety of ways.

1. **Objective:**
Overall content objective, *e.g.*, students will acquire the vocabulary, describing parts of the human body. Specific objective, *e.g.*, students will point to their eyes, nose, ears, mouth, hair. A picture file will also be used for this purpose.

2. **Motivation/Anticipatory Set:**
Teacher introduces topic by relating it to their background experience.

3. **Directed Instruction:**
Teacher directs lesson using puppet and models by asking puppet to point to his _____.

4. **Guided Instruction:**
Teacher guides students as students proceed through activity.

5. **Independent Practice:**
Students individually point to parts of their body.

6. **Alternate and Supplementary Activities**:
   ◆ Some may be able to carry out the teacher's role.
   ◆ Draw a picture.
   ◆ Use of interactive computer programs

7. **Evaluation/Summary/Closure**:
Use step 5 as evaluation by student pointing to eyes, nose, ear, mouth, hair.

Reading and Writing

No matter which reading approach is used, reading and writing should relate to the students' experience. Techniques using the Language Experience Approach include activities of the following types:

- Carry out an activity. Role play and discuss the experiences.
- Students dictate the event.
- The teacher writes the story on the board, or on butcher paper. The teacher reads the story to the children. Children read in a large group, small group, or individually.

Discussions and interactive activities preceding a reading experience can be incorporated into a Basal Reading Program to assure comprehension. Writing follows a similar student-based activity. In the case of young learners, children may only be able to draw on paper describing the activity. This is an important step, for it is the beginning of putting meaning on paper. Subsequently, they write their own stories, written within their developmental writing stages developing from scribbling to well formed letters.

These written projects can be sent home, placed in their portfolios, or displayed on bulletin boards. If early scribblings are sent home, there should be an attached note communicating to parents that learning to write involves a process and that the student work being sent home is not a finished product, but rather a reflection of the current process.

It is through oral presentation as well as by reading that comprehensible input can be made available. It is very important to provide meaningful communication as well many reading opportunities. Extensive reading throughout all levels adds to oral and writing skills. Initially pleasure reading should be emphasized. Early reading skills can lead to skills that will make it possible for students to read and appreciate the classics.

Culture

Modus operandi and artifacts of various cultures should be incorporated in the classroom. Holidays and special events should be acknowledged with discussion, and objects should provide a "hands-on" experience. The advantage is two fold. It provides an opportunity to demonstrate respect for other cultures, and also serves as a vehicle for use of the language being acquired.

A useful device a teacher can develop is a culture file. The culture file can contain pictures and written descriptions of events and objects that relate to various cultures. The file can be indexed by culture and by calendar event. To avoid stereotyping, it is best to have children initially speak about the special days or events related to their culture, than for the teacher to assume that all children of a particular culture are familiar with such days and events. Thus, the topic having been introduced, the teacher or class members can expand further through discussion.

A listing of cultural events, referenced to the twelve months of the calendar year, appears on the following four pages.

Respect for other cultures can be encouraged by inviting children to share cultural experiences with the class. These activities can be part of the classroom experience. Following are possible items and activities which students may offer.

- Photographs
- Games
- Pictures
- Costumes
- Art Objects
- Music
- Dancing

The teacher should use this interactive opportunity, for the child who performs or brings the objects

Special Days in the Multicultural Classroom
(based on current calendar; future years may differ slightly)

January

1	New Year's Day	14	New Year's Day (Roman Catholic)
	Emancipation Proclamation		Race Relations Day
	Cuba National Day	15	Martin Luther King, Jr. (Birthday)
	Haiti National Day		Humanitarian Day
	Sudan National Day	16	Religious Freedom Day
4	Burma National Day	20	Martin Luther King, Jr. Day (observed)
5	Kiribati National Day		Tu B'Shvar
6	Epiphany	22	Ukranian National Day
	Eastern Orthodox Christmas	26	Australia National Day
13	Togo National Day		Indian Republic
		27	Chinese, Korean, & Vietnamese New Year

February

1	Freedom Day: Anniversary	15	Susan B. Anthony's Birthday
	of the 13th Amendment		Nirvana Day (Mahayana Buddhism)
	to the U.S. Constitution	16	Lithuanian National Day
4	Sri Lanka National Day	16-22	Brotherhood/Sisterhood Week
	Chinese New Year (Monkey)	17	George Washington's Birthday (celebrated)
5	Mexican Constitution Day	18	Gambia National Day
	Boy Scout Sunday	22	George Washington's Birthday
6	New Zealand National Day		Saint Lucia National Day
9-15	National Crime Prevention Week	23	Brunei National Day
	(begins)		Guyana National Day
12	Abraham Lincoln's Birthday	24	Estonia National Day
14	Race Relations Day	25	Kuwait National Day
	St. Valentine's Day	27	Dominican Republic National Day

March

1	Welsh National Day	19	Purim
	Peace Corps Birthday	20	Tunisia National Day
3	Morocco National Day	21	Iranian New Year
4	Ash Wednesday		International Day of Elimination
6	Ghana National Day		of Racial Discrimination
8	International Women's Day		New Year (Afghanistan, Iran,
9	Eastern Orthodox Lent begins		Bah'a'i. Kurdish, Parsi)
10	Korean Labor Day	23	Pakistan National Day
12	Mauritius National Day	25	Greece National Day
14	Valentine's Day in Japan		Annunciation
17	St. Patrick's Day	26	Bangladesh National Day

April

4	Hungary National Day	18	Zimbabwe National Day
	Senegal National Day	19	Easter
	Idul-Fitr		Patriot's Day
5	Korean Arbor Day	22	Earth Day
8	Buddha Day (Mahayana Buddhism)	24	Armenian Martyr's Day
12	Palm Sunday	26	World Children's Day
13	New Year's Day (India, Nepal)		Easter Organization
14	Pan American Day		Tanzania National Day
16	Maundy Thursday	27	Afghanistan National Day
	Denmark National Day		Sierra Leone National Day
17	Good Friday	29	Japan National Day
	Kampuchea National Day	30	Israel National Day
	Syria National Day		Netherlands National Day
18	Pesach (Passover Begins)*		Yom Hashoah

May

1-7	Los Angeles Human Relations Week	14	Carabao Festival-Philippines
1	International Labor Day	17	Norway National Day
	May Day	18	Armed Forces Day
3	Japanese Children's Day		World Goodwill Day
	Poland Constitution Day		Victoria Day
5	Cinco de Mayo	20	Cameroon National Day
	Korean Children's Day	25	Argentina National Day
7	Yom Ha'atzmaut (Israel		Jordan National Day
	Independence Day)		African Freedom Day
8	Korean Parent's Day		Memorial Day
9	Czechoslovakia National Day	28	Ascension Day
10	Mother's Day	31	South Africa National Day
14	Paraguay National Day		

June

1	Tunisia National Day	10	Portugal National Day
	Western Samoa National Day	12	Philippine National Day
2	Italy National Day	14	Flag Day
4	Ascension Day (Eastern Orthodox)		Trinity Sunday
	Tonga National Day	17	Iceland National Day
5	Seychelles National Day	21	Father's Day
	Denmark Constitution Day	23	Luxembourg National Day
	World Environment Day	25	Mozambique National Day
6	Sweden National Day	26	Madagascar National Day
7	Shavout	27	Djibouti National Day
	Pentecost	30	Zaire National Day
	Chad National Day		

July

1	Burundi National Day	12	Sao Tomé & Pri'ncipe National Day
	Canada National Day	14	France National Day
	Rwanda National Day	17	Iraq National Day
2	Muharran (Islamic New Year)		Korean Constitution Day
4	U.S.A. National Day	20	Colombia National Day
5	Cape Verde National Day	21	Belgium National Day
	Venezuela National Day	22	Poland National Day
6	Comoros National Day 23		Egypt National Day
	Malawi National Day 24		Simon Bolívar's Birthday
7	Solomon Islands National Day	26	Liberia National Day
10	Bahamas National Day		Maldives National Day
	Race Unity Day	28	Peru National Day
11	Mongolia National Day	30	Vanuatu National Day
12	Kiribati National Day		

August

1	Switzerland National Day	15	Congo National Day
2	Islamic New Year		India Independence Day
3-9	City of Torrance Hungarian Festival		Korea National Day
4	Burkina Faso National Day	17	Gabon National Day
6	Bolivia National Day		Indonesia National Day
	Jamaica National Day	23	Romania National Day
8-16	Nisei Week	25	Uruguay National Day
9	Singapore National Day		Women's Equity Day
10	Ecuador National Day	31	Malaysia National Day
14	Pakistan Independence Day		Trinidad National Day
9	Czechoslovakia National Day		Tobago National Day

September

1	Libya National Day	15	Independence Day of Peace
2	Vietnam National Day	16	Mexican Independence Day
3	Qatar National Day		Papaua New Guinea National Day
4	Los Angeles' Birthday	17	U.S. Citizenship Day
6	Swaziland National Day	18	Chile National Day
7	Brazil National Day	21	World Gratitude Day
	Labor Day		Belize National Day
8	Andorra National Day	22	Mali National Day
	International Literacy Day	23	Saudi Arabia National Day
9	Bulgaria National Day	24	Guinea-Bissau National Day
12	Ethiopia National Day	26	Yemen National Day
15	Costa Rica National Day	27	Native American Indian Day
	El Salvador National Day	28	Rosh Hashanah (Jewish New Year)*
	Honduras National Day	30	Botswana National Day
	Nicaragua National Day		

October

1	Cyprus National Day	12	Sukkot
	Nigeria National Day		Spain National Day
	Korean Army Day		Dia de la Raza
	People's Republic of China		Equitorial Guinea National Day
	National Day		Columbus Day
2	Guinea National Day	20	Jewish Simchat Torah
3	German Unification Day	21	Somalia National Day
4	Lesotho National Day	22	Holy See National Day
5	Universal Children's Day	24	United Nations Day
	American Indian Awareness Week		Zambia National Day
	(begins)	26	Austria National Day
7	Yom Kippur*	27	St. Vincent & Grenadines Natl. Day
9	Korean Language Day	29	Turkey National Day
10	Republic of China National Day	31	Halloween
	Fiji National Day		All Souls Day

November

1	All Saint's Day	19	Monaco National Day
	Algeria National Day	22	Lebanon National Day
	Antigua & Barbuda National Day	25	Suriname National Day
	Day of the Dead		Religious Liberty Day
3	Panama National Day	26	Thanksgiving Day
	Dominica National Day	28	Mauritania National Day
	Election Day	29	Yugoslavia National Day
7	USSR National Day		Albania National Day
11	Veteran's Day	30	Barbados National Day
	Angola National Day		Benin National Day
18	Oman National Day		

December

1	World's Aids Day	12	Kenya National Day
	Central African Republic Natl. Day		Mexican Posadas
2	Laos National Day	15	Bill of Rights Day
	United Arab Emirates Natl. Day	16	Bahrain National Day
5	Thailand National Day	17	Bhutan National Day
	International Volunteer Day	18	Niger National Day
6	Finland National Day	20	Jewish Hanukkah*
7	Ivory Coast National Day	25	Christmas Day
10	Human Rights Day	26	Boxing Day—England, Ireland
10-16	Human Rights Week		Kwanza
12	Our Lady of Guadalupe Day	28	Nepal National Day

*date varies

may want to talk about their significance. Class discussion can be incorporated. A follow-up activity might be to discuss contributions from other cultures to strengthen the multicultural aspect of our society. Sometimes parents volunteer to come to class or to the school to contribute a cultural experience. An important point to keep in mind is that these classroom experiences help identify the child as special in a positive way, rather than as being different in a negative way.

Related to the topic of culture is the question of racial, ethnic, and religious identification. Discussion centered on geography sometimes leads to situations where children talk about the country of their origin. In some cases, children may be recent arrivals, or their families may have been in the United States for generations. To foster respect for the children's' perspectives about their identification it is best to have students voluntarily express their own identification. To illustrate, a Spanish-speaking child whose ancestry goes back to Mexico might call himself or herself:

- Latino(a)
- Chicano(a)
- Mexican
- Mexican American
- Hispanic
- American of Mexican Descent
- American

In the same way, a child may refer to himself or herself as Black, African-American, or multi-racial. The particular choice of these terms is very important to the child and to his or her family. In reference to the list above, it should not be surprising that a Spanish-speaking child would choose to identify himself/herself as American. In many cases parents at home discuss the questions dealing with identification. They talk about hardships encountered in the native country and remind family members that they are not foreigners in the United States, but Americans with full rights and responsibilities— Americans with a special underlying heritage.

In the multicultural society in which we live, it is a reality for a child to represent a combination of races and religions. Ii is suggested in the research literature that many minority and non-minority members of American society are in the process of defining their views and beliefs and are in no position to declare their specific identity. Here we have presented some of the reasons for allowing children to call themselves whatever they wish, rather than for a teacher to expect a child to fit the teacher's definition.

In the context of a multicultural society, general mainstream artifacts and *modus operandi* should be introduced, *e.g.*, national holidays, honoring events, heroes, birthdays, Mother's Day, etc. An additional advantage that cultural recognition affords is that students can handle objects, talk about events, and add to the classroom language experience.

Classroom Management Ideas

With respect to classroom management, it is important that teachers make sure that students know the rules and behavior expectations from the beginning of their classroom experience. Rules should be carefully discussed to assure that these rules are understood. Students can re-state the rules in their own words, act them out, participate in games in which rules are reviewed, and, in the early grades, draw pictures illustrating a rule, *e.g.*, raising your hand to ask permission to speak, etc. The rules can be numbered so that the teacher can occasionally refer to the number to remind students. The teacher can say the number or indicate it by the use of her/his fingers.

It is important to formalize as many classroom procedures as possible so that the classroom management procedures are predictable to the students, *e.g.*, line-up, class dismissal, appropriate noise level, putting away materials, monitor rules, etc.

It is also important for teachers to assure that they are being fair, consistent, and firm, so as to enable students to acquire a sense of security in the classroom.

Assistant Participation in the Classroom

It is a fortunate situation for the teacher and students when an assistant is assigned to a class. Whoever the assistants may be, it is important that they be used effectively. The first step is to prepare training materials with which to tutor the classroom assistant.

The materials, best prepared in booklet form, should include:

Role of Assistant:
- ◆ Provide natural communication contexts for children. Accept language variation, but model standard forms to ensure that children are adding this important linguistic option to their repertoire.
- ◆ Be supportive to the students. Be friendly. Introduce yourself and know students' names.
- ◆ Praise a child and use appropriate modeling procedures.
- ◆ Know how to deal with behavior problems.
- ◆ What is the role of the teacher in regard to the responsibility of the classroom? What are teacher responsibilities? What are assistant responsibilities?
- ◆ Know how to handle information with confidentiality, *e.g.*, medical problems.

School Orientation:
- ◆ Know the school and class schedule.
- ◆ Know the names of school staff and support staff.
- ◆ Be familiar with school map indicating parking, eating, bathroom, supply room areas, etc.
- ◆ Know the school regulations, *e.g.*, time of arrival, departure, etc.

To help cope with the diversity of students and class size it has become increasingly important to enlist trained individuals from the community as classroom assistants, particularly to work with small groups. On occasion the assistants may be older students in the same school, *e.g.*, fifth graders helping third graders. Learning centers can also be of great value by providing appropriate practice on an individual or small group basis. When there is no assistant available, the centers are even more indispensable.

Parents in the Classroom

Another important addition to the classroom is parent participation. The participating parents may not necessarily be the parents of children in the class, since such assignments will be at the discretion of the teachers and school administration.

There is a growing diversity in our school population today, and as expected that diversity is even more pronounced in our second-language classrooms. In the case of English-as-a-Second-Language classrooms, the diversity is represented by many different cultures. In bilingual programs there is often a great deal of diversity even within one language group. In the Spanish language component, for example, there can be children from Mexico, Central America, Spain, South America, and Puerto Rico—all with unique cultural assets.

Thus, parents should be encouraged to participate in the classroom. Involving parents is one way to tap the cultural resources that the students bring to the school experience, *e.g.*, story telling, music, songs, dancing, cooking, drawing, pointing, etc.

It is important to acknowledge the need for parent support by first recognizing the value of all home cultures:

- ◆ Remind parents that they are the children's first and most influential teacher and role model.

- ◆ Point out the importance of the children's first language. By telling stories, myths, reading aloud in the children's first language, the parent adds linguistic, cultural, and cognitive enrichment. That will benefit the child and add to our country's linguistic and cultural resources.

- ◆ Tell parents that learning new labels in English is a relatively easy transfer task, if children have already learned a concept in the first language.

♦ Conceptual subject matter learned in the first language is a great advantage in attaining success in school subjects in the second language, and at the same time adding to self-esteem.

There are many ways to involve parents in the class. In some schools, parents come to the classroom on a regular basis, encouraging a social climate which promotes cooperation and self-esteem for the child. In some schools, parents come during the first and last hour of instruction of the school day. They assume a place in the routine of the class, particularly by helping with small-group instruction. In these classes, where parents play such a role, the most common result is a positive educational direction for the entire classroom.

When a problem arises concerning a child's behavior and a parent is addressed by the teacher, it is important to keep the following in mind:

♦ Begin the conversation with positive comments, *e.g.*, "It is a pleasure to see that Bob is always on time." "Sally is very attentive."

♦ When you discuss the problems, have suggestions in mind, not orders, that you and the parent can accept as mutual solutions.

♦ Listen to parents.

♦ Keep in mind that you have a professional obligation to create an empowered classroom for every child in the classroom.
Inform students and their parents of the advantages that bilingualism provides:

♦ In addition to acquiring English and the American culture, the student already possesses a first language within a framework of its culture. Bilingualism adds depth to the life experience of the student and supports the connection to his/her heritage. No less important, the bilingual students and their language add to the country's linguistic resources, which are becoming more important as the country becomes more concerned with expanding international commerce.

♦ Research points out that bilingualism provides a cognitive dimension beyond that provided to the monolingual. In the second chapter, a study is described in which bilinguals, though initially not as proficient in English, upon reaching high school were at the same level or higher than their monolingual peers.

These bilingual assets should be stated to students and parents, for they provide an important base upon which to expect high performance from students acquiring a second language.

Homework

In planning homework for language acquisition classes, it is important to incorporate into the homework assignments tasks that draw upon the resources that the family and their primary culture provide, such as:

♦ Stories, folktales, songs, and riddles from the primary culture.

♦ Interviews with parents about the home culture or country of origin.

♦ Family life in this country, *e.g.*, family birthplace parties, family members, family tree.

Homework assignments involving subject matter in the second language should be a low anxiety activity, through which children practice what they have already learned in the classroom. Assignments should be carefully explained, so students can complete the tasks without frustration. Homework should not require parental help unless the teacher has previously communicated with parents and provided a structure for such parental involvement.

ESL and Special Education

Special Education students are usually not able to function in a regular classroom due to disability or handicap. Nonetheless, with modification, the suggested techniques, methods, and approaches described in this text apply equally well to such students. Critical components which underlie instruction must be kept in mind:

♦ **Comprehensible input**: Students must comprehend instruction.

♦ **Low affective filter**: Special attention should be devoted to motivation, self confidence, and keeping anxiety at a low level. Special attention should be devoted to promoting self-esteem.

Instruction should meet the special needs of these special learners:

1. Age: Ages may vary with the class and not correspond to mental maturity normally associated with the chronological age, *e.g.*, an 18-year-old may perform at first-grade level.

2. The number of disabilities represented in the class may be numerous.

3. The degree to which a student is disabled will also vary.

Assessment procedures should play a key role to ensure that students:

1. Have been properly identified.

2. Have been identified as having disabilities or physical handicaps but not wrongly classified because they are in the process of learning English as a second language.

3. May reach a level where they can function in a regular classroom.

A primary goal of instruction should be to equip these special student population with social-survival skills:

1. Getting along with peers.

2. Survival in the community.

3. Conforming to the conventions of general society.

4. Functioning as citizens of our nation.

Parental support will also vary:

1. Some parents will accept their child as being special and will be supportive.

2. Some will be in a state of denial of their child's disability.

3. Some will not be able to support their child due to their own disabilities.

4. Some parents and their children may feel disassociated from each other, *e.g.*, the deaf child because communication differs from the norm may feel he or she is a member of a different culture.

Adult Education

With modifications, the techniques, methods, and approaches described previously also apply to adult learners. Necessary modifications should be influenced by the following:

1. Adults usually have well-defined goals, *e.g.*, high school diploma, employability, job improvement, social communication, etc.

2. Focus on survival skills needed in a new country, *e.g.*, renting, buying a house, shopping, medical help, legal questions related to driving a car, etc.

3. The need for culture skills to survive in a new country, *e.g.*, getting along with other groups than their own, asking questions, defending oneself, civil rights, etc.

4. Adult classes tend to be heterogeneous in regard to:

- ◆ Age.
- ◆ Home language: Many home languages may be represented in the classroom and some students may speak several languages.
- ◆ The students' repertoire of experiences will far exceed their English-language skills.
- ◆ Some will work full time; others may be homemakers with children.
- ◆ Attendance may be irregular due to outside responsibilities.
- ◆ Some may have disabilities.

5. The teacher will have to improvise techniques to meet the needs of adult students who, accustomed to print, want to read early.

- ◆ Prepare easy-to-read materials, *e.g.*, paraphrase current newspaper articles.

6. Have students role-play situations related to their immediate survival needs and goals.

Special attention should be devoted to the use of picture files, sheltered English/SDAIE techniques, cooperative learning, role playing, and other procedures particularly suited to an adult student audience.

Teaching English As A Foreign Language (TEFL)

The key difference between English-as-a-Second-Language (ESL) and English as Foreign Language (EFL) is the societal setting in which the course is taught to non-English speakers. The role of the teacher in an EFL class is to provide extensive and effective opportunities to develop listening, speaking, reading, and writing skills in English in a country in which English is not the primary language.

Expected EFL Teacher Competencies

Following are the competencies expected of an EFL teacher:

- ◆ Knowledge of the role of theory in EFL instruction.
- ◆ Use of appropriate practice supports made available in most classrooms, *e.g.*, bulletin boards, picture files, learning centers, etc.
- ◆ Understanding of the differences between ESL and EFL.
- ◆ Understanding of the instructional requirements of EFL and ESL classes.
- ◆ Development of the role of the teacher in an EFL class.
- ◆ Development of instructional plans for EFL classes for listening, speaking, reading, writing, and cultural understanding.
- ◆ Demonstration of effective methods and techniques for teaching EFL.
- ◆ Practical knowledge of programs, approaches, methods, and techniques for foreign-language teaching.
- ◆ Effective lesson planning for teaching a foreign language: listening, speaking, reading, and writing.
- ◆ Role of grammar—teaching grammar in foreign language classes.
- ◆ Development of an EFL portfolio to use as a resource.
- ◆ Incorporating cognitive levels into EFL instruction.

Relevant Topics for The EFL Teacher

The EFL teacher will focus on the following major topics:

1. Comprehensible input, affective filter.
2. EFL in an educational context.
3. Design of instructional materials.

4. Design of tutorial materials.
5. The Language Experience Approach (LEA) and reading and writing.
6. Formal and informal assessment.
7. Current methodologies as related to EFL, TPR, the Natural Approach, Sheltered English/ Specially Designed Academic Instruction in English, cooperative learning, etc.
8. EFL and sociopolitical, economic, and institutional context as part of an overall educational context.

The following sections and topics in this book relate to TEFL competencies:

- Introduction
- Theory
- Bulletin boards
- Flannel boards
- Picture file
- Thematic units
- Assessment
- ESL in bilingual programs
- Sheltered English/SDAIE
- The Natural Approach
- Teacher proficiency in student's L1
- Comprehensible input and low affective filter
- Reading and writing
- Culture
- Classroom management
- Assistants and parents in the classroom
- Homework
- Special education
- Adult education
- Glossary

Legal Basis for ESL/Bilingual Education

Bilingual Education Act of 1968: Bilingual Education has been debated since the founding of our country, but with the Bilingual Education Act of 1968 the needs of language-minority students were addressed by national policy. However, the Act did not specify the goal as to whether bilingual education was to be a remedial or enrichment effort. In a remedial perspective, speakers of languages other than English are viewed as being in need of overcoming a language deficiency. This approach is also known as the deficit model. In contrast, in the enrichment perspective a language other than English and its associated culture are viewed as an asset to the student and society in general.

Under the 1968 Act, implementation decisions relative to bilingual education were left to local school districts, resulting in varying interpretations of appropriate educational treatments. Differences in demographic composition of communities, scarcity of bilingual teachers, and federal and state politics have added to the challenge of providing the needed instruction for minority-language students. Parental concerns have frequently resulted in lawsuits. The two legal cases described below are indicative of the need for school reform.

Serna vs. Portales Municipal Schools: This lawsuit in 1972 resulted in the ordering of instruction in a child's first language and culture.

Lau vs. Nichols: This case resulted in a ruling by the United States Supreme Court based on the rights of language-minority students, granting special assistance to enable them to participate in the school program. The ruling stated that equal treatment, that is, providing the same mainstream curriculum to all, was not sufficient. The old sink or swim approach, or submersion, was no longer acceptable.

The debate concerning bilingual education and its effectiveness continues. Due to the difficulty of controlling the many variables involved, it has been very difficult to evaluate its effectiveness. A more recent approach to the debate has been to apply the findings from basic research coupled with school experience and then view results from a longitudinal perspective. Basic research takes into account such factors as self-esteem, cultural value as well as the individual value to society, and such variables as bilingualism as a cognitive asset.

Continuity in Empowerment

As the title of this chapter suggests, this has hopefully served as an introduction to and description of the many ways by which the second-language classroom can be empowered. Topics can be added and those presented here can be expanded. It is hoped that teachers will use the best available theory, apply such ideas, and couple them with their professional judgment and personal experience toward creating the empowered classroom.

An important conclusion hopefully reached from reading this chapter is that teaching approaches used in second-language instruction are not too different from good teaching practices used in mainstream instruction. An important distinction is that, in classes where students already speak the language of instruction, meaning can be assumed, while in classes where a second language and a second culture are being acquired, meaning cannot be assumed. Methods concerned with comprehension, maintaining a low anxiety level, and recognizing cultural considerations are indispensable.

Finally, another important set of skills indispensable to effective second-language teaching involve assessment:

♦ Students must be assessed to determine which ones will benefit from various forms of instruction in a particular class.

♦ Diagnostic assessment must be a part of the instruction to assure that students are receiving appropriate instruction.

♦ Assessment must assure that students are ready to enter mainstream instruction when they demonstrate the appropriate skill levels.

Acronyms/Glossary

Basic Terms

ESL	English as a Second Language
EFL	English as a Foreign Language
SSL	Spanish as a Second Language
_SL	any language as a Second Language

Student Designation

LEP	Limited English Proficient
ELL	English Language Learner
	(both terms apply to the same student)
FEP	Fluent English Proficient
EO	English Only
ELDP	English Language Development Program

Theoretical Terms

L1	Native Language, Home Language
L2	Second Language
BT	Bloom's Taxonomy. Different levels of cognitive skills:

1. **Knowledge**, *e.g.*, name people/animals in the story;
2. **Comprehension**, *e.g.*, tell story in your own words;
3. **Application**, *e.g.*, if you were_____, what would you do?

4. **Analysis**, *e.g.*, which part of the story surprised you or frightened you?

5. **Synthesis**, *e.g.*, tell, role play, write the story from the point of view of _____.

6. **Evaluation**, *e.g.*, did _____ make the correct decision?

BICS	Basic Interpersonal Communicative Skills (takes 2-3 years to acquire)
CALP	Cognitive Academic Language Proficiency (takes 5-7 years to acquire)
CUP	Common Underlying Proficiency

Programs in which a second language is taught:

Bilingual programs:
- ◆ Maintenance
- ◆ Two-Way Enrichment
- ◆ Transitional (Early/Late Exit)
- ◆ Immersion (Canadian Model)

Non-bilingual programs:
- ◆ Pull-Out
- ◆ English Language Development (ELD)
- ◆ Submersion (Sink or Swim) — outlawed

Assessment

SOLOM	Student Oral Language Observation Matrix
CARE	Criteria for Addition of Reading in English
(pre)LAS	(pre)Language Assessment System
LAB	Language Assessment Battery
BSM	Bilingual Syntax Measure
BINL	Basic Inventory of Natural Language

Approaches/Strategies

LEA — Language Experience Approach. Student-centered reading approach using background experience, vocabulary, and language patterns which have been internalized previous to the reading experience.

BASAL — A reading approach characterized by systematic organization of reading instructional materials: teacher guides, manuals, scope, and sequence charts.

SEA/SDAIE Sheltered English Approach/Specially Designed Academic Instruction in English (Both names apply to academic instruction in English). SDAIE better describes instruction which focuses on academic instruction rather than on language development.

TPR — Total Physical Response. Used appropriately throughout a program to assure comprehension.

NA — Natural Approach. Stages: Preproduction, Early Production, Speech Emergence, Intermediate Fluency.

Organizations

CABE	California Association for Bilingual Education
NABE	National Association for Bilingual Education
CAFABE	California Association for Asian Bilingual Education
TESOL	Teachers of English to Speakers of Other Languages
CATESOL	California Association of Teachers of English to Speakers of Other Languages
AMAE	Association of Mexican American Educators
NAME	National Association for Multicultural Education

References

These texts are useful to teachers of a second language; some contain extensive bibliographies:

Banks, J. (1989). *Multi-Ethnic Education: Theory and Practice*. Boston, MA: Allyn & Bacon.

Board of Human Relations Commissioners (1992). *Discover the Real New World: Human Relations in Los Angles*. Los Angeles, CA: Human Relation Commission.

Canter, L. & M. Canter (1991). *Parents on Your Side*. Santa Monica, CA: Lee Center & Associates.

Canton-Harvey, G. (1987). *Teaching ESL in the Content Areas*. Reading, MA: Addison-Wesley.

City of Los Angles Human Relations Commission (1992). *Ethnic Calendar*. Los Angeles, CA: Board of Human Relations.

Crandell, J. (ed.). (1987). *ESL Through Content Area Instruction*. Englewood Cliffs, NJ: Prentice-Hall

Crawford, J. (1989). *Bilingual Education: History, Politics, and Practice*. Third Edition. Los Angeles, CA: Bilingual Education Services, Inc.

Cummins, J. (1984). The Role of Primary Language Development in Promoting Educational Success for Language Minority Students. *Schooling and Language Minority Students: A Theoretical Framework*. Office of Bilingual-Bicultural Education, California State Department of Education. Los Angles, CA: Evaluation, Dissemination and Assessment Center, California State University, Los Angeles. pp. 3-49.

Cummins, J. (1989). *Empowering Minority Students*. Sacramento, CA: California Association for Bilingual Educators.

Enright, D.S. & D.L. McCloskey (1988). *Integrating English: Developing English Language and Literacy in the Multilingual Classroom*. Reading, MA: Addison-Wesley.

Epstein, J. (1983). *How Do We Improve Programs for Parent Involvement*. Baltimore, MD: Johns Hopkins University Center for Social Organization of Schools.

Hanson, R., J. Bailey, & H. Molina. (1981). The Implications of Intra-Program Placement Decisions for the Understanding and Improvement of Schooling. *Studies in Educational Evaluation*, 7, 2, 193-211.

Holt, D., (ed.) (1993). *Cooperative Learning: A Response to Cultural Diversity*. Washington, DC: Center for Applied Linguistics.

Krashen, S. & T.D. Terrell. (1983). *The Natural Approach*. Oxford, United Kingdom: Pergamon Press

Krashen, S. (1987). *Principals and Practice in Second Language Acquisition*. Englewood, NJ. Prentice-Hall.

Krashen, S. & D. Biber. (1988). *On Course: Bilingual Education in Success in California*. Sacramento, CA: California Association of Bilingual Education.

Molina, H. (1976). An Assessment System in an Instructional Program Designed for Spanish-Speaking Children. *System: A Journal for Educational Technology and Language Learning Systems,* 4, 40-46.

Molina, H. (1975). The Need and Function of Built-In Assessment Instruments in Instructional Programs Designed for Spanish-Speaking Children Learning English. *The Journal of Instructional Psychology*, 2, 4, 14-18.

Molina, H. (1975). Evaluating the Effectiveness of a Program Used in School Situations Characterized by High Pupil Absenteeism and Attrition. *System: A Journal for Educational Technology and Language Learning Systems*, 3, 48-54.

Molina, H. (1974). Assessment in an Instructional Program Designed for Spanish-Speaking Children Acquiring English Language skills. ERIC ed 930-910. Abstract in *Research in Education,* November.

Molina, H. (1971). Language Games and the Mexican-American Child Learning English. *TESOL Quarterly*, 5, 145-148.

Molina, H. (1976). *Development of the SWRL English Language and Concepts Program for Spanish-Speaking Children: A Monograph*. Los Alamitos, CA: SWRL Educational Research and Development.

Ovando, C. & V. Collier. (1985). *Bilingual and ESL Classrooms*. New York: McGraw-Hill.

Terrell, T. (1986). Acquisition in the Natural Approach: The Binding/Access Framework. *The Modern Language Journal*, 4 (10), pp. 213-217.

Notes

▼2▼
Early Reading Instruction, Non-English-Language Background, and Schooling Achievement

By Huberto Molina, Donna Farrell Siegel, and Ralph A. Hanson

Introduction

This chapter presents the results of two related studies that examine the relationship among early reading instruction, non-English-language background, and the schooling achievement of high school seniors. Collectively, these studies challenge the current thinking about when students should begin receiving formal reading instruction and that being from a non-English-language background (NELB) is generally synonymous with being academically disadvantaged.

An earlier study, the Kindergarten Reading Follow-up (KRF) Study, provided the data source for these two inquiries. The KRF Study was a national follow-up study of a kindergarten beginning-reading program carried out with a grant from the United States Department of Education. The purpose of the study was to examine the long-term effects on high school seniors of learning to read in kindergarten (Hanson & Siegel, 1988a). Accordingly, data were obtained on those high school seniors who had received formal beginning reading instruction in kindergarten, as well as on others who had comparable educational experiences, but had not been taught to read until first grade.

The NELB Kindergarten Reading Follow-up Study further analyzed the data from the KRF Study. Specifically, it looked at the reading achievement of NELB students. This study began with the knowledge from the KRF Study that those students who were taught to read in kindergarten, as opposed to those who began such instruction in first grade, were better readers as high school seniors and had less need for remediation during both elementary and secondary grades. While these same results emerged when students were examined by ethnic background, gender, and social class populations, the NELB student population had not specifically been examined. Hence, this study sought to determine if these same results could be generalized to NELB students.

Results from this research supported the finding from the original KRF study. That is, like other students, the NELB students who began their reading instruction at the kindergarten level were better readers and needed substantially less remediation than those who did not. However, it also raised questions about the overall level of achievement of NELB students. This issue was the focus of a second study, The NELB Schooling Achievement (NSA) Study.

The goal of the NSA Study was to determine if high school seniors from NELB families had different overall schooling achievement levels than those from English-language backgrounds (ELB). Using global measures of schooling achievement, the overall achievement of NELB students at both the elementary and secondary levels was compared to that of their ELB peers.

Both of these studies are described in the sections that follow. However, since the KRF Study was the source of the original data-base, a brief description of the methods, procedures, and major related finding of that study are presented first.

The Kindergarten Reading Follow-up (KRF) Study

Currently, there is little agreement about the optimum time to begin formal reading instruction with children. Some research has suggested that four- and five-year-old children who learn to read maintain their advantage over those children learning at later periods in their lives (*e.g.*, Durkin, 1968; Mason, 1984; Beck, 1987). Others argue that such children are exceptions and that there is really no advantage in learning to read early. Still others insist that learning to read at an early age will have long-term negative effects (Rudolph & Cohen, 1984). They recommend that formal reading instruction should begin around six-and-a-half years of age, or about the time the child's first permanent teeth appear.

Collectively, today's kindergarten and school-entry policies reflect this same ambivalence (*e.g.*, Bennet, 1986) and the result is a dramatic difference in the ages at which students begin receiving formal reading instruction in our nation's schools. While some children begin receiving reading instruction as early as four years of age, others are as old as eight before such instruction begins. Does this difference in the age at which children begin receiving formal reading instruction have any effect on their subsequent schooling experiences, reading achievement, attitudes, and literacy levels as young adults?

Using extensive and unique data sources resulting from longitudinal research efforts spanning nearly twenty years, the KRF Study examined this issue of when, how, and to whom formal reading instruction should be provided. Specifically, the research sought to answer two questions: (1) Are there any long-term effects associated with receiving formal reading instruction in kindergarten?; and (2) Are there any special effects for disadvantaged students of receiving this instruction?

A series of national evaluation studies carried out in the early 1970s had documented the progress made by each class, school, and district that participated in a kindergarten Beginning Reading Program (BRP) (*e.g.*, Hanson & Schutz, 1978). Hence, a large, descriptive database was compiled on the early reading ability of students from over 2,000 elementary schools in 400 districts across the country. The accessibility of this extensive database made it possible to conduct a detailed follow-up study during the 1985-86 school year.

Conducting the KRF Study

Conducting the KRF Study required the completion of three related groups of tasks. One set of tasks was the design, development, pilot testing, and final preparation of the data collection instruments. This set of tasks resulted in the development of three instruments: The Reading Biographer, The Reading Vocabulary Test, and the comprehension items from the *Academic Instructional Measurement Systems*. All three instruments were incorporated into a single sixteen-page data collection pamphlet called the *Student Booklet*.

A second set of tasks was securing the participants and gathering the follow-up data. This involved identifying the BRP follow-up schools and districts, orchestrating the various activities required to obtain and maintain their participation, and doing the actual data collection and data entry.

A third and final set of tasks was the formulation of the study design, analysis of the data, and documentation of the results. In the following sections, the procedures followed to complete each task are summarized. A more complete account of each task is given in Hanson and Siegel (1988a).

The three data-collection instruments were designed to accomplish two objectives. The first was to carefully assess the students' reading ability as high school seniors. This was accomplished through the use of two instruments:

- A standardized test of reading comprehension, the *Academic Instructional Measurement System (AIMS)* developed by Sabers (1958) and used with permission of the Charles Merrill Publishing Company.

- A specially developed test of reading vocabulary (Broach, Hanson, & Siegel, 1988).

A second objective for the study instrumentation was to assess other factors in students' experiences related to their reading competence as high school seniors. Over the course of one full year, a self-report questionnaire, referred to as *The Reading Biographer,* was developed for this purpose (Hanson & Siegel, 1988b). *The Reading Biographer* measures the major events in a child's life, from preschool through high school, that are related to the development of reading competence in the areas of home, school, and extracurricular activities (Siegel, 1987; 1990).

Participants and Study Design

A large and representative sample of 3,959 participants provided data from high school seniors across the country who had entered specific elementary schools in 1973-74. They were obtained from a total of twenty-three BRP school districts and one non-BRP district in ten different states representing all regions of the country. The vast majority of the elementary schools represented had been designated as Title 1-eligible and served disadvantaged populations in 1973-74. Only 252 students, or 16 percent of the total BRP sample, were from non-Title 1 schools. In the original kindergarten BRP inquiries, the overall sample of participating schools included a slightly larger sample of Title 1 students; this was considered desirable since a major objective of the BRP Follow-up Study was to assess the effects of the kindergarten reading effort with at-risk student populations.

In addition to data from these high school seniors, the study contained the careful documentation of each elementary school's efforts and degree of success in teaching kindergarten children to read using the BRP during the 1973-74 school year (Hanson & Schutz, 1976). This baseline information could be used to categorize those students who attended kindergarten in the elementary schools which implemented the BRP into various comparison groups. However, the full follow-up study sample included many high school seniors who were not in this category. Specifically, there were those who: (1) attended BRP elementary schools but not for kindergarten (*i.e.*, entered in first grade or later); or (2) attended some other elementary school (usually in the same district) that did not implement the BRP in kindergarten. Collectively, these differences in the students' kindergarten and elementary experiences allowed for the formation of different comparison groups that facilitated the study objectives.

The information was used to create two designs. In Design 1, there were three comparison groups defined as follows: (1) those who *did not* attend one of the BRP schools (*i.e.*, assumed *not* to have received formal reading instruction in kindergarten); (2) those who began attending a BRP school in some grade above kindergarten (*i.e.*, assumed to have the same or similar elementary school experiences as the kindergarten BRP students, but did not take part in the kindergarten BRP); and (3) those who began attending a BRP elementary school in kindergarten and therefore received the BRP instruction (See Design 1 in Figure 1).

Design 2 was also comprised of three comparison groups, which more precisely examined the students in category 3 in Design 1 (See Design 2 in Figure 1). The three comparison groups in Design 2 are defined as follows: (1) those who *did not receive* kindergarten reading instruction (*i.e.*, categories 1 and 2 in Design 1); (2) those who *received some* kindergarten reading instruction (*i.e.*, from 8 to 10 units); and (3) those who received the full BRP program in kindergarten. These groups provide a more rigorous comparison since two of the groups received at least some kindergarten reading instruction. Here the expectation would be that group 1 would provide the baseline measure, group 2 would show some effects, and group 3 would show the maximum difference on the effects variables. As with Design 1, the results were evaluated using both a one-way ANOVA and two-way ANOVA, with the high school attendance center being the second main effects factor.

Figure 1:
Number of Students and a Description of Each KRF Study Design Comparison Group

Design 1 Comparison Categories:

Kindergarten Experience Categories

No kindergarten BRP/ No BRP elementary school	No kindergarten BRP/ Attended a BRP elementary school	Kindergarten BRP/ Attended a BRP elementary school
n=1161	n=871	n=1453

Note: In both designs, student is the unit of analysis and all students are included. High School is used as a control factor in the two-way ANOVA.

Design 2 Comparison Categories:

Kindergarten Experience Categories

No Kindergarten BRP	Some Kindergarten BRP	Most/All Kindergarten BRP
n=2425	n=443	n=1091

Note: In both designs, student is the unit of analysis and all students are included. High School is used as a control factor in the two-way ANOVA.

Major Related Findings of the KRF Study

The students from the twenty-four school districts and ten states which provided follow-up data are described in terms of their gender, ethnic/racial categories, and socioeconomic background in Table 1. As these data show, there were slightly more males than females and the sample was quite diverse in terms of ethnic and social-class background. In terms of ethnic background, minority groups comprise about 40 percent of the total sample, with Hispanic students accounting for about .03 percent of this total.

As might be anticipated, the social-class background data show somewhat larger proportions in the lower and middle categories than the population at large. This is consistent with their representation in the original kindergarten BRP studies, where lower SES groups and minorities were also over-represented. Overall, these descriptive statistics show the diversity expected in a large sample of high school seniors.

Another important descriptive aspect of the follow-up sample is the extent to which students who

Table 1
Description of KRF Study Participants
by Gender, Ethnic/Racial, and Socioeconomic Background

Factor	Categories	Number	Percentages
Gender	1 Females	1,888	48.0
	2 Males	2,049	52.0
Ethnic Background	1 Asian	303	8.3
	2 Black	687	18.8
	3 Hispanic	110	3.0
	4 Native American	375	10.0
	5 All Others	2,177	59.5
Social Class	1 Lowest	428	11.0
	2 Lower Middle	1,070	27.5
	3 Middle	1,430	36.8
	4 Upper Middle	711	18.3
	5 Highest	245	6.3

Table 2
The Number of Students, High Schools,
and Districts Included in the Full KRF Study Sample

Kindergarten/Elementary School Categories	Students No.	Percent	High Schools	Districts
No BRP or BRP Elementary School	1,549	39	41	23
No BRP/some BRP Elementary School	867	22	42	23
BRP and BRP Elementary School	1,534	39	41	23
No Information	9	—	—	—
Totals	3,959	100	43	24

received the kindergarten BRP reading instruction in 1972 are represented. Some data on this issue are given in Table 2.

This summary gives the number of students, high schools, and districts providing follow-up data by the three kindergarten/elementary school categories. As the Table 2 indicates, the high schools and districts provided data on students who had quite different kindergarten and elementary school experiences. There were 1,549 (39 percent) seniors in the first category: those who did not receive the kindergarten BRP and did not attend an elementary school that offered it (*i.e.*, they either attended another elementary school in the same district, or transferred into the district after elementary school). In the second category, there were 867 (22 percent) high school seniors. The seniors in this category did not receive the kindergarten BRP, but did attend an elementary school that offered it (*i.e.*, they enrolled in a BRP elementary school sometime after kindergarten). The third category contained 1,534 high school seniors (39 percent); the seniors in this category were the ones who both attended a BRP elementary school and received the kindergarten BRP instruction. The fourth and final category included nine seniors for whom no information was available on their elementary and kindergarten experience.

The substantial number of high school seniors in the first three categories was considered a positive result; these three categories, as well as the sub-categories within each, would provide the basis for forming the student groups used for comparison purposes in evaluating the effects variables.

The analysis within both designs showed clear and consistent support for teaching reading in kindergarten. Participation in a systematically-developed and carefully-implemented kindergarten reading program was related, not only to higher reading skills, but to higher performance on all indicators of reading competency. Further, students from schools completing more of the BRP were better readers as high school seniors when compared to those from schools completing only a portion of the program. In comparing the kindergarten-reading students to other students in their same district who did not receive any kindergarten reading instruction, the results were even more conclusive. Learning to read in kindergarten was not only related to higher reading skills, but it reduced the need for remediation at both elementary and high school levels. Students receiving the kindergarten-reading instruction fared better in all ways than those who did not receive the instruction; these results were consistent across districts and by racial/ethnic, gender, and socioeconomic groups.

The NELB Kindergarten Reading Follow-Up Study

The methodology used in the KRF Study allowed for a closer examination of the three kindergarten-reading comparison groups to see if the finding could be generalized to specific sub-populations of interest. One such population was the NELB students. Hence, these students were the focus of the NELB Kindergarten Follow-Up Study. This study examined the policy issue of whether or not it was advantageous for schools to provide formal reading instruction in English to NELB children in kindergarten.

The debate taking place in both the research and policy arenas concerning the timing and methods used to present formal reading skills to children from NELB families is even more complex than that for English-language background (ELB) students (*e.g.*, Garcia, 1987). Here the debate centers around not only the age at which formal reading instruction should begin, but also whether it should be in the student's native language or in an "English only" format.

One of the difficulties in researching both of these issues is that most research cannot afford the luxury of taking a longitudinal/developmental approach. As a result, most studies are of short duration and critics can dismiss any successful efforts by saying the effects obtained are probably temporary and will dissipate, or perhaps even turn negative, over time. In essence, it is difficult to find studies with data that (a) can operationally define both the type and timing of students' initial formal reading instruction and (b) have follow-up data documenting the achievement of students involved in such programs at a later point in time (*e.g.*, at the end of their formal schooling). Since the KRF Study database fulfilled both of these criteria, analyses could be carried out that would provide some insights into this debate.

In the NELB Study, three of the dependent variables from the KRF Study were evaluated for those students who were self-defined as speaking English-as-a-second language (ESL); that is, those students who reported that a language other than English was the dominant language spoken in the home by both the parents *and* the children. Figure 2 describes the three dependent variables. For each of these variables, an analysis of variance (ANOVA) was computed to compare results for students in the three kindergarten reading experience categories: (1) No kindergarten reading instruction, (2) some kindergarten reading instruction, and (3) much/all kindergarten reading instruction. The results appear in the following section.

What Did We Learn?

There were 496 students or 12.5 percent of the full study sample (N=3,959) designated as non-English-background (*i.e.*, from homes in which *both* parents and children regularly spoke a language other than English). About one-half of these students spoke a European language other than Spanish; about one-third spoke Spanish, and the remainder were in the "Asian" and "other language" categories.

Table 3 reports the results of the three NELB kindergarten reading comparison groups. Overall, the results show that kindergarten reading instruction was a significant factor for two of the three dependent variables: "Remedial Experiences" and "Reading Comprehension." Looking at the three comparison groups for "Remedial Experiences," we see that the students who received the full kindergarten reading instruction had 14 percent fewer students in remedial classes as compared to those who had none and 4 percent fewer than those who had received only part of the instruction. This has important economic as well as educational implications for school districts, since providing remediation is not only costly, but largely ineffective and highly related to drop-out rates. Thus, school districts can estimate the dollar amount saved in remediation costs alone by reducing remediation by 14 percent.

Table 3:
ANOVA Results for the Three Dependent Variables
by Kindergarten Beginning Reading Program (BRP) Categories for NELB Students.

	Dependent Variables		
Kindergarten BRP Categories	Remedial Experiences	Vocabulary	Reading Comprehension
No Kindergarten BRP	.32 (n=286)	16.1 (n=292)	11.6 (n=290)
Some Kindergarten BRP (1-7 units)	.22 (n=36)	16.2 (n=36)	13.0 (n=36)
Most/All Kindergarten BRP (1-10 units)	.18 (n=164)	17.0 (n=168)	13.2 (N=167)
p level	.01	.08	.00

Figure 2:
Dependent and Independent Variables and Coding Descriptions.

Independent Variables:

Social Class:	Social economic class:
	    1 = Low.
	    2 = Middle.
	    3 = High.

Language:	Dominant language spoken by both parents and student in the home:
	    1 = Foreign.
	    2 = English.

Dependent Variables:

Reading Comprehension:	Score obtained on the AIMS norm-referenced reading test: Range = 1 - 20.
Reading Vocabulary:	Score obtained on a norm-referenced vocabulary test: Range = 1 - 25.

Independet Variables:

Reading Stage:	Chall reading stage categories:
	    1 = 3rd-5th-grade reading level.
	    2 = 5th-7th-grade reading level.
	    3 = 7th-10th-grade reading level.
	    4 = 10th-12th-grade reading level.

Elementary Remediation:	Number of years attended remedial class and/or held back in grades 1-6:
	    1 = No remediation.
	    2 = 1 year in remedial classes and/or held back one year.
	    3 = 2 years in remedial classes and/or held back 2 years.
	    4 = 3 or more years in remedial classes or held back 3 years or more.

Secondary Remediation:	Number of years attended remedial class and/or held back in grades7-12:
	    1 = No remediation.
	    2 = 1 year in remedial classes and/or held back one year.
	    3 = 2 years in remedial classes and/or held back 2 years.
	    4 = 3 or more years in remedial classes or held back 3 years or more.

Elementary Achievement:	Usual grade received in reading and usual yearly school attendance in grades 1-6:
	    1 = Low achievement.
	    2 = Average achievement.
	    3 = Above-average achievement.
	    4 = Superior achievement.

Secondary Achievement:	Usual grade received in English and usual yearly school attendance in grades 7-12:
	    1 = Low achievement.
	    2 = Average achievement.
	    3 = Above-average achievement.
	    4 = Superior achievement.

Kindergarten Reading:	Participation in a beginning reading program in kindergarten:
	    1 = Did not participate in a beginning reading program in kindergarten.
	    2 = Participated in a beginning reading program in kindergarten.

Family Size:	Number of people in the immediate family:
	    1 = 2 people in family.
	    2 = 3 people in family.
	    3 = 4 people in family.
	    4 = 5 people in family.
	    5 = 6 people in family.
	    6 = 7 people in family.
	    7 = 8 or more people in family.

Turning to the "Reading Comprehension" variable, once again, the unlikely result observed in the KRF Study emerges again. That is, the NELB students from the Title 1 schools (*i.e.*, "disadvantaged") scored significantly higher than those from the non-Title 1 schools (*i.e.*, "advantaged"). Also, as with the other two variables, we see that the mean score is higher for those students who received most or all of the reading instruction in kindergarten than for those who received only part of the instruction. These findings suggest that providing NELB students with an English-speaking program of beginning reading instruction at an early age is both appropriate and effective. Furthermore, the more of this kind of instruction, the better readers they will be as adults.

Although the third variable, "Vocabulary," was not statistically significant in the ANOVA, the mean scores clearly follow the same consistent pattern of increase associated with each of the three levels of kindergarten reading implementation. That is, the mean score was highest for those students who received all of the instruction and lowest for those students who did not receive any kindergarten reading instruction.

By examining the separate means for all of these variables (within each cell of the ANOVA), one can clearly see that the NELB students who received the kindergarten reading instruction showed clear patterns of higher vocabulary and reading comprehension scores and required less remediation as seniors in high school than those who did not receive the early reading instruction. This is an exceptional finding, and particularly important since those students receiving the early reading instruction were from a *lower* social class background than those not receiving it. Consistent with a poorer SES background, children from those homes would also be expected to have *less* language background and experience in any language (*i.e.*, either their native language or English).

Also significant is the finding that the mean scores for all three effects variables were higher for the students who received most or all of the kindergarten reading instruction than for those who only received a portion of the program. Being able to relate such subtle implementation differences to an educational intervention over a short-tern period would be unusual; being able to discern such effects over a period of twelve years can only be called astounding.

In summary, the results of the analysis presented in this study provide support for the conclusion that the positive effects of beginning formal reading instruction in kindergarten generalize to NELB children. This is, consistent with the findings for other population groups, those NELB students who began receiving their formal reading instruction in English at the kindergarten level had fewer remedial experiences and better vocabulary and reading comprehension scores as seniors in high school than those NELB students who did not.

The NELB Student Achievement (NSA) Study

The findings of the NKF Study supported providing reading instruction in English to kindergarten students from NELB families. Further, a more detailed analysis of the high school achievement variables showed that the NELB students actually showed better results, as a group, than the ELB students in several areas (Hanson, Molina, & Siegel, 1988). Hence, a second study, the NELB Student Achievement (NSA) Study, sought to further examine this general issue of NELB student achievement. The goal of this study was to determine if being from a NELB was an advantage or disadvantage to overall school achievement.

There is little agreement about the effects of non-English-language background on the schooling achievement of children (Hakuta & Pease-Alvarez, 1992; Lewelling, 1991). In fact, much of the early research contended that having a non-English-language background could have a harmful effect on children's intellectual development (*e.g.*, Yoshioka, 1929; Smith, 1931, 1939; Anastasi & Cordova, 1953). More recent studies, however, have suggested that a having a non-English-language backgrounds may actually be beneficial to cognitive ability (Peal & Lamber, 1962; Ben-Zeev, 1977; Duncan & DeAvila, 1979; Goldsmat, 1982; Cummins, 1982). Still, many educators, parents, and policymakers argue that a non-English-language background hinders the mastery of English and, therefore, the ability to do well in school and, eventually, the work place (*e.g.*, Youth Policy, 1983; Crawford, 1989).

The NELB Student Achievement Study sought to provide further insights into this debate. Using the Kindergarten Reading Follow-up (KRF) Study database, this study examined the schooling achievement of children from NELB homes and compared them to similar samples of children from ELB homes. The purpose was to determine if children who have had the experience of growing up with a NELB would display achievement levels that were below, the same, or higher than their ELB peers from comparable social class background.

Method of Examining Two Linguistic Groups

To examine this issue, the students were divided into two major groups based on their linguistic background: (1) Non-English-language background (*i.e.*, a language other than English was the dominant language spoken in the home by both the parents and the children), and (2) English-language background (*i.e.*, English was the *only* language spoken in the home). Measures obtained on each of nine dependent variables (seven achievement and two background) for NELB students within each of three social-class categories (low, middle, and high) were compared with the scores obtained by the monolingual students within each of these same social class categories. These nine variables and their descriptions are provided in Figure 2.

This study used seven variable measuring achievement; three of these variable were measures of either reading achievement or vocabulary. The "Reading Comprehension" variable consisted of scores obtained on the Aims Instruction Measurement System (AIMS). "Reading Vocabulary" was a measure of the students' vocabulary and was obtained from the theory-driven *Reading Vocabulary Test,* which was specifically developed to provide stable, interpretable estimates of respondent vocabulary size (Hanson & Siegel, 1988b; Borach, Hanson, & Siegel, 1988).

Both of these reading tests conformed to the requirements for the formulation of another reading achievement variable, "Reading State." This variable categorized students' reading skills into one of five different categories, based on the Chall model of reading stages (Chall, 1983).

Four other achievement variables were measures of general school achievement. "Elementary Remediation" and "Secondary Remediation" measured the number of years the students participated in remedial classes and/or were held back in elementary and high school. "Elementary Achievement" and "Secondary Achievement" categories measured student achievement in terms of the student's usual grade in reading or English and the number of days missed each year in school.

The last two variables included in this study, "Kindergarten Reading" and "Family Size," were background variables which previous studies had indicated contribute to students' overall school achievement. The "Kindergarten Reading" variable measured whether or not the students participated in a beginning reading program in kindergarten. Since this variable was a significant factor in the reading achievement of NELB students as well as the overall sample, it was considered to be an important variable to consider in this study. "Family Size" measured the number of people in the student's immediate family. Overall, children from larger families tend to do less well in school than those from smaller ones; thus, this was considered another important variable to examine.

Results of Overall Reading Comprehension

Each of the dependent variables was evaluated for the two language experience groups via descriptive statistics and a two-way ANOVA procedure. Then the separate means for each of the variables (within each cell of the ANOVA) were reviewed. Together they showed consistent results regarding the long-term achievement levels of NELB students, as compared to ELB students. The complete two-way ANOVA results for one of the dependent variables, "Reading Comprehension," is presented in Table 4. A summary of the results for all nine variables, including the cell means, are given in Table 5.

The results in Table 4 show that, as far as overall reading comprehension at the twelfth-grade level is concerned, there was no statistical difference between the tow groups. That is, the fact that the students were NELB did not appear either to contribute to, nor detract from, their overall level of reading achievement as measured on a norm-referenced reading ability test. This was somewhat surprising, since this is an English-language test. The fact that the NELB students did not score lower on an English test of general reading comprehension is comparable to English-speaking students taking a test in a second language and scoring about the same as students who speak that language fluently.

In fact, as Table 5 indicates, only three of these seven variables showed any differences between the

Table 4
Two-Way ANOVA Breakdown for One Dependent Variable: "Reading Comprehension"

Source of Variation	DF	Sum of Sq.	Mean Sq.	f	Sig.f
Main Effects	3	629.8	202.9	14.10	0.000
Social Class	2	580.4	290.2	19.50	0.000
Language	1	44.3	44.3	3.30	0.084
2-way Interaction					
Social Class and Language	2	18.4	9.2	0.62	0.538
Explained	5	648.2	129.6	8.70	0.000
Residual	3,018	44,867.1	14.6		
Residual	3,023	45,515.3	15.1		

Table 5
Summary of Two-Way ANOVA Results
(Bilingual/Monolingual and Three Social-Class Categories)
for the Nine Dependent Variables.

Dependent Variables	Bilingual Students			Monolingual Students			
	Low SES (n=149)	Mid SES (n=92)	Hi SES (n=14)	Low SES (n=1580)	Mid SES (n=999)	Hi SES (n=190)	Sig. f
Reading Comprehension	12.60	12.80	13.60	13.00	13.10	14.90	0.084
Reading Vocabulary	15.20	16.10	18.00	17.10	17.10	20.90	0.000
Reading Stage	2.60	2.70	3.00	2.80	2.80	3.40	0.634
Elementary Remediation	0.33	0.33	0.07	0.30	0.33	0.19	0.821
Secondary Remediation	0.25	0.28	0.07	0.25	0.33	0.19	0.903
Elementary Achievement	2.80	2.70	3.10	2.70	2.70	3.00	0.606
Secondary Achievement	2.40	2.40	3.30	2.40	2.40	2.90	0.995
Kindergarten Reading	1.47	1.52	1.38	1.38	1.40	1.35	0.002
Family Size	4.30	4.40	4.00	4.00	3.80	3.70	0.000

NELB and ELB populations: "Reading Vocabulary", "Kindergarten Reading", and "Family Size." All of these would logically be expected to show a difference in mean scores. Vocabulary, which is a component of reading ability, is largely impacted by the home and family environment (Anderson, *et al.*, 1985). Thus, students who speak and use only English at school and through extra-curricular activities would be expected to have less of an English vocabulary than students using English in these settings and also at home.

Table 5 also indicates that more of the NELB students participated in a kindergarten beginning reading program. Since this is Title III program and implemented largely in schools with disadvantaged populations, this is also to be expected. This probably means that the number of NELB students who participated in a kindergarten beginning reading program was larger from poorer families than the ELB students who participated in the same program. It is important to recall, however, that the earlier studies showed that participating in this program was related to students' overall level of school achievement. Therefore, it is possible that this one factor may have had an impact on the mean scores of the achievement variables in this study.

Finally, the vast majority of the NELB students in the study come from Hispanic and lower social-class populations. Since these populations tend to have more children than the comparison population, the mean for the NELB population would be expected to be higher for this variable.

More unexpected is the fact that all of the other six variables, which measure school achievement, show no difference between the two groups. Furthermore, by examining and comparing the mean scores on these variables within social-class categories (*e.g.*, low ELB with low NELB), one can see that the scores on the NELB students in the high social class categories show even a slight advantage over the ELB students in the same category. Although this difference is not enough to be statistically significant, it does mean that, on average, the NELB students from more advantaged homes had less remedial experiences and higher levels of achievement, both in elementary and in high school, than the ELB students. However, as might be expected, the two reading achievement scores, "Reading Comprehension" and "Reading Stage," were slightly higher for the ELB students.

This study supports bilingual programs, for they build on the students first-language skills. Once concepts are attained, it is possible to efficiently transfer such skill into English. Sheltered English-language programs as components of a bilingual program are designed to accomplish this transfer task.

Bilinguals add to the country's resources by providing linguistic and cultural assets to the expanding international nature of commerce. These findings suggest that schools should express high expectations for children who come from bilingual families, for these students bring with them cognitive values attributed to bilingualism.

Summary

The results of the analyses presented in this study provide useful information concerning the progress, over time, of NELB students in our schools. They indicate that these students are generally not at a disadvantage in terms of standard educational measures taken in high school. That is, after controlling for social-class and family size, having a non-English-language home background has no negative effects on the general achievement levels of children.

One variable shown to contribute to the overall achievement levels of both NELB and ELB students in earlier studies was participating in a beginning reading program in kindergarten. This study showed that significantly more NELB students participated in this program than ELB students. Thus, as noted earlier, this variable may have affected the mean scores on the other variables. Thus, this variable should be examined further, possibly by carrying out an analysis of covariance to determine if, indeed, participating in a kindergarten reading program did impact the other achievement variables.

The earlier-reported NKF Study found that the positive effects of early reading instruction did generalize to NELB children. The second study reported here extended these results by showing that when the effects of students' social-class background are taken into account, being from a NELB has little or no relationship to higher overall levels of school achievement. It should be noted that school achievement is operationally defined here by variables which are all very clearly limited to English-language competence. Thus, such factors should be expected to favor students with English-language backgrounds. However, this did not emerge. NELB students achieved at very comparable levels. Thus, being from a non-English-language background had no direct relationship to students' school achievement. However, if broader measures of achievement were used, including perhaps other language/cultural measures, a positive relationship may emerge for NELB students.

Policy Implications

This chapter summarizes the results of the KRF Study and presents analysis from two related studies focusing on the NELB students in that larger study. The analysis within all three study designs showed:

◆ Clear and consistent support for teaching reading to all children in kindergarten.

Participation in a systematically developed and carefully implemented kindergarten reading program was related not only to higher reading skills, but to higher performance on all indicators of reading competency. Further, students from schools completing more of the kindergarten BRP were better readers as high school seniors as compared to those completing only a portion of the program. In comparing the kindergarten reading students to other students in their same district who did not receive any kindergarten reading instruction, the results were even more conclusive. Learning to read in kindergarten was not only related to higher reading skills, but it reduced the need for remediation at both the elementary and high school levels. Students receiving the kindergarten reading instruction fared better in all ways than those who did not receive the instruction. Moreover, these results were consistent across districts, and by racial/ethnic, gender, socioeconomic, and NELB groups. In all comparisons, the kindergarten reading students clearly emerged as better off than those who did not receive the instruction.

◆ Students from non-English-language backgrounds are very comparable to English-language background students (*i.e.*, are not necessarily academically disadvantaged as often portrayed).

The popular notion that NELB students are necessarily at a disadvantage because of their background was not supported. To the contrary, the results indicated that NELB students, particularly those provided with early reading instruction in English, in this case, are *not* disadvantaged based on six types of standard educational measures taken at the end of high school. That is, after controlling for social class and family size, being from a NELB has no negative and may, indeed, have positive effects on the general achievement levels of children.

◆ Follow-up study and other longitudinal approaches to teaching and programs appear to be methodologies to use in future studies of schooling effects.

The studies reported here illustrate this point. Though simplistic when compared with the full set of possibilities that a full information system methodology would present, these approaches clearly define schooling effects more precisely than those provided by other methods.

Although schools are generally not able to provide data on the programs and experiences of students who progress through them, such a capability is emerging rapidly in some districts. Schools and other social service institutions are improving in their ability to handle information. Accordingly, better and more complete resources for policy information on schooling should emerge in the near future. Such information can then be used to routinely monitor the long-term effects of given practices and programs such as kindergarten reading, both within and across districts (Hanson & Siegel, 1991).

The extraordinary findings in these studies indicating superior reading competency being associated with receiving reading instruction in kindergarten, examined across districts and schools, as well as ethnic, gender, socioeconomic, and NELB groups, provides the strongest possible support for such methods and information systems.

References

Anastasi, A. & Cordova, F. (1953). Some Effects of Bilingualism Upon the Intelligence Test Performance of Puerto Rican Children in New York City. *Journal of Educational Research, 44,* 1-9.

Anderson, R.C., Hiebert, E.H., Scott, J.A., & Wilkerson. I. (1985). *Becoming a Nation of Readers: The Report of the Commission on Reading.* Urbana, IL: University of Illinois. Center for the Study of Reading.

Beck, J. (1986). *How To Raise a Brighter Child.* New York: Pocket Books.

Bennett, W.J. (1986). *First Lessons: A Report on Elementary Education in America.* Washington, DC: U.S. Department of Education.

Ben-Zeev, S. (1977). The Influence of Bilingualism on Cognitive Strategy and Cognitive Development. *Child Development, 48,* 1009-1018.

Broach, D., Hanson, R., & Siegel, D. (1988, April). Estimating Vocabulary Size: An Example of Function Specific Test Development. Paper presented at the National Council on Measurement in Education, New Orleans, LA.

Chall, J. (1983). *Stages of Reading Development.* New York: McGraw-Hill.

Crawford, J. (1989). *Bilingual Education History, Politics, Theory, and Practice.* Trenton, NJ: Crane Publishers.

Cummins, J. (1982). *Tests, Achievement, and Bilingual Students.* Rosslyn, VA: National Clearing House for Bilingual Education.

Duncan, S.E. & DeAvila, E.A. (1979). Bilingualism and Cognition: Some Recent Findings. *NABE Journal, 4,* 15-50.

Garcia, E. (1987). Bilingualism Development and the Kindergarten Child. Paper presented at the annual meeting of the American Educational Research Association, Washington, DC.

Goldsmat, M. (1982). Follow-up Studies in Bilingual Education: Issues and Options. In J. Gage (Ed.). *Longitudinal Studies in Second Language Learning and Bilingual Education.* Washington, DC: National Clearinghouse for Bilingual Education.

Hakuta, K. & Pease-Alvarez, L. (Eds.). (1992, March). Special Issue on Bilingual Education. *Educational Researcher, 21* (2).

Hanson, R., Molina, H., & Siegel, D.F. (1988, April). Kindergarten Entry Age, Bilingual Background, and Early Reading Instruction as Factors in the Reading Competence of High School Seniors. Paper presented at the annual meeting of American Educational Research Association, New Orleans, LA.

Hanson, R., & Schutz, R.E. (1975). *The Effects of Programmatic R & D on Schooling and the Effects of Schooling on Students: Lessons from The First Year Installation of the SWRL/Ginn Kindergarten Program.* Technical Report 53. Los Alamitos, CA: Southwest Regional Laboratory for Educational Research and Development.

Hanson, R. & Schutz, R. (1978). A New Look at Schooling Effects from Programmatic Research and Development. In D. Mann (Ed.), *Making Change Happen?* (pp. 120-149). New York, NY: Columbia University Press.

Hanson, R. & Siegel, D.F. (1988b). Design and Development of the Reading Biographer: An Application of Function Specific Assessment. Paper presented at the annual meeting of the National Council on Measurement in Education, New Orleans. LA.

Hanson, R. & Siegel, D.F. (1988a). *The Effects on High School Seniors of Being Taught to Read in Kindergarten.* Technical Report 1. Garden Grove, CA: Hanson Research Systems.

Mason, J. (1984). Early Reading From a Developmental Perspective. In D. Person (Ed.), *Handbook of Reading Research* (pp. 505543). New York: Longman.

Lewelling, V.W. (1991, February). Academic Achievement in a Second Language. *Eric Digest* (Report No. EDO-FL-91-01). Washington, DC: ERIC Clearinghouse on Languages and Linguistics, Center for Applied Linguistics.

Pearl, E. & Lambert, W.E., (1962). The Relation of Bilingualism to Intelligence. *Psychological Monographs. 76* (27. Whole No 546).

Rudolph, M. & Cohen, D. (1984). *Kindergarten and Early Schooling.* 2nd ed. Englewood Cliffs, NJ:

Prentice-Hall.

Sabers, D. (1985). *Curriculum Test of Mastery: Technical Report.* Columbus, OH: Charles Merrill.

Siegel, D.F. (1987). Identification and Validation of Process Factors Related to the Reading Achievement of High School Seniors: A Follow-Up Study. Unpublished doctoral dissertation, The University of Tulsa, Tulsa, OK.

Siegel, D.F. (1990, July/August). The Literacy Press: A Process Model for Reading Achievement. *Journal of Educational Research, 83* (6), 336-347.

Smith, M.E. (1931). A Study of Five Bilingual Children from the Same Family. *Child Development, 2,* 184-187.

Smith, M.E. (1939). Some Light on the Problem of Bilingualism as Found From a Study of the Progress in Mastery of English Among Pre-school Children of Non-American Ancestry in Hawaii. *Genetic Psychology Monographs, 21,* 119-284.

Yoshioka, J.G. (1929). A Study of Bilingualism. *Journal of Genetic Psychology, 36,* 473-479.

Youth Policy, (1983, June). Issue/Debate: Proposed Fiscal 1984 Reductions in Bilingual Education.

Notes

▼3▼

Confronting "Unalterable" Background Characteristics of English-Language Learners

By Huberto Molina, Donna F. Siegel, and Ralph A. Hanson

Introduction

The environmental studies of Bloom (1964) and Hunt (1961) firmly established that early childhood is the most critical period for an individual's intellectual growth and development. Furthermore, as researchers began to examine "process" or "alterable" variables (*i.e.*, the particular behaviors that are under the direct control of parents and educators) rather than "frame" or "unalterable" variables (*e.g.*, social class, ethnic background, number of children in the family), they discovered that the specific kinds of educational experiences that parents and teachers provide for children can make a significant difference in the students' school achievement levels (Majoriebanks, 1979; Bloom, 1984; Bennett, 1986).

Although the evidence accumulated over the past several decades consistently confirms that literacy development and school achievement are linked to children's early educational experiences (Hanson & Siegel, 1988; Siegel, 1990), these studies have not specifically examined the preschool educational experiences of children from a non-English-language background (NELB). Moreover, there is little agreement about the factors impacting the school achievement of NELB children. Some research has suggested that children from NELB have an academic advantage over those from English-language backgrounds (*e.g.*, Goldsmat, 1983; Cummins, 1982) while others contend that such children are at a disadvantage (Crawford, 1989).

What is in agreement from the research to date, however, is that a disproportionate percentage of NELB children have difficulty in school (*e.g.*, poor grades, high dropout rates, low levels of English literacy). As with other children experiencing difficulties in school, the problems often appear at the beginning of their formal school experiences (usually in kindergarten) and increase over time. In many instances, the achievement status of NELB children is unclear due to the differences in English-language competence.

However, in spite of the language differences, many NELB children are able to achieve at average or superior levels (*i.e.*, the early pattern of difficulty in school never materializes). Thus, it would seem that a logical area to examine for possible reasons for the differential success of NELB children would be differences in their early childhood experiences.

This chapter presents research that pursues this goal by identifying particular early childhood process variables related to the later school achievement of NELB children. An earlier study found that specific preschool educational experiences for English-language-background students were highly related to achievement levels in both elementary and in secondary school (Siegel, 1990). This was considered an extraordinary finding, since only broad measures of early educational experiences were obtained, yet the results showed that, more than twelve years later, these early experiences had a significant relationship to the students' school achievement.

Would this same finding hold true for NELB students? The purpose of this study was to address this question and determine what specific preschool educational experiences (*i.e.*, birth through age 6) of NELB students were related to their reading, vocabulary, remedial experiences, and literacy level as seniors in high school. Identifying these factors would provide a model for the kinds of preschool educational experiences that parents and teachers should provide for NELB children to ensure later success in school.

Method

The study employed a follow-up design which included obtaining a sample of students from an original population of students from over 5,000 elementary schools, in 430 districts across the country, that had used an innovative kindergarten reading program in the 1973-74 school year (Hanson & Schutz, 1978). In 1985, a sample of the 430 original kindergarten reading program districts were contacted and asked to take part in a follow-up study (Hanson & Siegel, 1988a). This effort resulted in obtaining a follow-up sample of 3,959 high school seniors, from twenty-eight school districts, representing all regions of the United States. Finally, the data from students reporting that they were from NELB families were identified and selected to analyze for this study. The analysis of these data allowed for the examination of the research question, "What preschool process variables are related to the later school achievement of NELB students?"

Study Instrument

The major study instrument used was The Reading Biographer. This instrument was specifically designed to measure the home, school, and extracurricular experiences of students from birth through high school (Hanson & Siegel, 1988b). It was prepared especially for this purpose and includes detailed information on the students' family background, language use, and early home and educational experiences. Two other instruments, a standardized reading comprehension test and a reading vocabulary test, were also used in the study. All three of these instruments were completed by each high school senior in the follow-up study and provided the data used for this study.

Description of the NELB Sample Population

The 339 NELB high school seniors in this study (8.5 percent of the full follow-up sample) are from the 28 districts that participated in the earlier follow-up study and provide the necessary variability in terms of the major study variables of interest. These NELB students were from homes in which the students reported that both parents *and* children regularly spoke a language other than English. About one-half of these students spoke a European language other than Spanish, about one-third spoke Spanish, and the remainder were in the Asian and other language categories. These data allowed NELB students' early childhood home and educational experiences to be analyzed in terms of which preschool educational produced the highest levels of school achievement.

Study Variables

Four dependent variables, measuring school achievement across a student's development, and four independent variables, measuring the particular educational experiences that were provided by parents and teachers during the students' preschool years, were computed. These variables are presented in Figure 1. What is important to note here is that all of the independent variables are process variables. That is, they are all variables controlled by parents, teachers, or school districts and, hence, are important for developing policy in the area of NELB early childhood education.

**Figure 1
Description of Study Variables**

Early Childhood Process (Independent) Variables:

KPRG — Whether or not the student participated in the SWRL kindergarten Beginning Reading Program (BRP) (*i.e.*, was provided formal beginning reading instruction) in kindergarten.

    1 = No   2 = Yes

PSCATS — Number of home educational activities the student participated in BEFORE kindergarten. These educational activities included:
- Reading books alone or with parent(s).
- Parent(s) reading student bedtime stories.
- Learning nursery rhymes.
- Watching *Sesame Street*.
- Using crayons and coloring books.
- Playing word and number games.

    1 = low   2 = moderate   3 = High

PRESCH — Whether or not the student attended preschool classes BEFORE kindergarten.

    0 = No   2 = Yes

EAGE — Age of the student upon entering his/her senior year in high school.

    1 = 17 years old or younger: Student is a young age for grade level.
    2 = 17.1-18 years old: Student is an average age for grade level.
    3 = 18.1 or older: Student is an older age for grade level.

High School Achievement (Dependent) Variables:

REMED — Number of remedial classes in which the student was enrolled during elementary and high school.

    0 = None   1-3 = 2   4+ = 3

PSTAGE — Whether or not the student was classified as functionally illiterate (*i.e.*, reading at or below the 5th grade level according to Chall's five reading stages) as a senior in high school.

    0 = Not classified as functionally illiterate.
    1 = Classified as Functionally illiterate.

VSCRCATS — Student's vocabulary test score category.

    1 = low   2 = Moderate   3 = High

RDGCATS — Student's reading comprehension test score category.

    1 = low   2 = Moderate   3 = High

Table 1 provides the descriptive statistics for each of the study variables as well as the number of NELB students in each category.

Table 1 Descriptive Statistics for the Study Variables			
Study Variables	n	Mean	S.D.
Participated in the Kindergarten Reading Program (KPRG)	No = 186 Yes = 153	1.45	.498
Home Educational Activities (PSCATS)	High = 43 Average = 198 Low = 71	1.91	.599
Preschool Attendance (PRESCH)	No = 229 Yes = 110	.324	.025
Senior Year in High School Entry Ages (EAGE)	17 & younger = 124 17.1 to 18 = 130 18.1 & older = 27	1.65	.648
Number of Remedial Classes Enrolled in During Grades K-12	None = 222 1 to 3 yrs. = 82 4 or more yrs. = 28	1.41	.642
Vocabulary Test Score Category (VSCRCATS)	High = 44 Average = 248 Low = 47	1.99	.519
Reading Comprehension Test Score Category (RDGCATS)	High = 94 Average = 155 Low = 88	2.01	.736

Using ANOVA procedures, each of the four dependent school-achievement variables were evaluated in terms of the four preschool educational experiences. By examining the mean scores on the dependent variables (within each cell of the ANOVA), it can then be determined which of the early educational experiences of NELB students are associated with high and which are associated with low school achievement as high school seniors.

Results

Results of the analyses carried out on this NELB population confirm the same findings as for the English-language-background students: specific early educational experiences are related to the school achievement of NELB students. By examining the patterns of the mean scores in each category of the early childhood process variables, as well as their relationship (*i.e.*, significance level) to the school-achievement variables, the specific preschool educational experiences that affect long-term achievement levels of NELB students emerge. These results are shown in Table 2.

Table 2
Relationship of the Early Childhood Process Variables
to the School-Achievement Variables

		School Achievement Variables			
Early Childhood Process Variables	Categories	Remedial Classes (REMED) n x Sig.	Vocabulary (VSCRCATS) n x Sig.	Reding Comprehen. (RDGCATS) n x Sig.	Functional Illiteracy (PSATGE) n x Sig.
Participated in the Kindergarten Reading Program (KPRG)	No Yes	180 1.49 .01 152 1.32	186 1.9 NS 153 2.0	185 1.9 .00 152 2.1	184 .24 .02 152 .14
Home Educatioal Activities (PSCATS)	High Average Low	43 1.30 NS 194 1.42 69 1.41	43 2.2 .00 198 2.0 71 1.7	42 1.9 .05 197 2.1 71 2.2	42 .05 .00 197 .14 71 .32
Attended Preschool (PRESCH)	No Yes	223 1.41 NS 109 1.42	229 2.0 NS 110 2.0	228 2.0 NS 109 2.1	227 .22 .03 109 .13
Senior Year in High School Entry Age (EAGE)	Young Average Older	121 1.32 NS 129 .133 25 .140	124 2.0 .00 130 2.1 27 1.7	123 2.2 .03 130 2.1 27 1.7	122 .16 .00 122 .13 27 .44

As these data indicate, those NELB students that participated in a kindergarten beginning reading program had higher reading-comprehension scores, needed less remediation, and had fewer students classified as functionally illiterate as seniors in high school. This indicates that NELB students would benefit significantly in each of these achievement areas simply by beginning a program of formal reading instruction in kindergarten. The only achievement variable in this study that was not affected by the kindergarten reading program was the students' vocabulary score.

The amount of home educational activities provided by the parents before the child attended kindergarten also had a major impact on later schooling achievement. The results imply that the more preschool educational activities that the student participates in, such as learning nursery rhymes and stories, reading books, watching *Sesame Street*, and playing work and number games, the greater the students' vocabulary, reading comprehension, and literacy level at the end of high school. Although these activities did not show a relationship to the need for remedial classes, the mean score for those in the "high" category shows that, overall, this group had less need for remedial classes than those in either the "average" or "low" category. These results indicate that those parents who want their children to do well in school must take the time to ensure that their children engage in these kinds of activities during their preschool years.

Attending preschool shows a strong relationship to literacy level but to none of the other process variables. This variable probably has some commonality with "Home Educational Activities" since it includes only those students who were either enrolled in a preschool and/or took special lessons such as music, dance, swimming, or Sunday school; it did not include daycare. These kinds of structured educational experiences typically include some kind of formal instruction as well as many of the activities that are included in the "Home Educational Activities" variable. Once again, these results point to the importance of providing NELB students with diverse, formal educational activities during their preschool years.

The last process variable, "Senior Year in High School Entry Age," also indicates a strong relationship to three of the school achievement variables: vocabulary, reading comprehension, and illiteracy. It shows that those students who were young for their grade level had higher levels of achievement than both those who were average and older for their grade level. This finding needs to be examined further, since it has not been determined why some of these students were older. For example, were they older because they started school late (*i.e.*, entered kindergarten when they were 6 rather than 5 years of age) or were they held back a year? The same is true for those classified as "average" age for their grade level. Were they "average" because of the school district's cut-off date for school entry (*i.e.*, August or September 1st vs. December) or because they started at an early age and were later held back? Whatever the reason, one thing is quite clear: those students who were young for their grade level as seniors in high school outperformed their older peers on all of the school achievement variables. Although the need for remediation shows no relationship to this age variable, the means still show that those students who were young for their grade needed less remediation than those who were older.

The sample kindergarten population in this follow-up study participated in schools twenty years ago. Since that time, several types of educational programs designed for NELB students have been placed in operation in our nation's schools. Researchers in the field, consistent with our findings, recommend bilingual programs that make maximum use of language and concept-forming activities that provide maximum transfer effects from the native language to the second language. Maintenance bilingual and two-way immersion programs are recommended. These programs support the valuable resources of culture and language. In the two-way immersion program, speakers of the minority language and speakers of English are schooled together and all emerge bilingual, yet attain grade level or above proficiency in both languages (Cummins, 1993).

Conclusions

The results of the analyses presented in this chapter provide useful information concerning the kinds of early childhood experiences and interventions parents, teachers, and schools need to provide for NELB students in order to foster higher levels of student achievement in elementary and high school. Collectively they indicate that early educational experiences are essential to NELB students for success in school. These experiences include participating in home educational activities such as those described in Figure 1, beginning formal reading instruction no later than kindergarten, attending preschool, entering school at an early age, and not being held back. One conclusion that must be drawn from this study is that the more of these kinds of early educational experience that NELB students have, the more successful they will be in their later school years.

This study reconfirms the conclusions of the early environmental studies of Bloom and Hunt. That is, the "unalterable" background characteristics of children associated with poor school performance (*e.g.*, low SES, NELB) can actually be "altered" through early educational experiences. For example, a recent survey by the National Center for Educational Statistics showed that over 60 percent of high-income parents had their 3- and 4-year-old children enrolled in prekindergarten programs as compared to only 30 percent of low-income parents (National Center for Educational Statistics, 1993).

Thus, a second conclusion that can be drawn from this study is that, given at least comparable preschool educational experiences, the achievement gap between the "unalterable" frame variables of non-English-language-background and English-language-background should narrow significantly. Since the kinds of educational experiences that parents and teachers provide for children at an early age have been shown to impact their later achievement levels, early childhood educators and schools should be providing these experiences for *all* children, not just those in the upper social class.

Earlier studies have found that particular alterable early childhood experiences are positively related to later school achievement for English-language-background students and that early reading instruction in English is one factor that generalizes to NELB student achievement. This study shows that other alterable early childhood variables, such as early home educational experiences or formal preschool education (English or otherwise) also generalize to NELB students.

References

Bloom, B.S. (1964). *Stability and Change in Human Characteristics*. New York: John Wiley.

Bloom, B.S. (1984). The New Direction in Educational Research: Alterable Variables. *Phi Delta Kappan*, 61, 382-385.

Chall, J. (1983). *Stages of Reading Development*. New York: McGraw-Hill.

Crawford, J. (1989). *Bilingual Education: History, Politics, Theory, and Practice*. Trenton, NJ: Crane Publishers.

Cummins, J. (1993). Empowerment through Biliteracy. In *The Power of Two Languages*. New York: Macmillan/McGraw-Hill.

Cummins, J. (1982). *Tests, Achievement, and Bilingual Students*. Rosslyn, VA: National Clearing House for Bilingual Education.

Goldsmat, M. (1982). Follow-up Studies in Bilingual Education: Issues and Options. In J. Gage (Ed.), *Longitudinal Studies in Second-Language Learning and Bilingual Education*. Washington, DC: National Clearing House for Bilingual Education.

Hanson, R.A., Molina, H. & Siegel, D.F. (1988). Kindergarten Entry Age, Bilingual Background, and Early Reading Instruction as Factors in the Reading Competence of High School Seniors. Paper presented at the annual meeting of the American Educational Research Association, New Orleans, LA, April 5-9.

Hanson, R.A. & Schutz, R.E. (1978). A New Look at Schooling Effects from Programmatic Research and Development. In D. Mann (Ed.), *Making Change Happen?* New York: Columbia University Press.

Hanson, R.A. & Siegel, D.F. (1988a). *Effects on High School Seniors of Learning to Read in Kindergarten*. Technical Report #1, Garden Grove, CA: Hanson Research Systems.

Hanson, R.A. & Siegel, D.F. (1988b). Design and Development of the Reading Biographer: An Application of Function Specific Assessment. ERIC Document Reproduction Service No. ED 324 356 TM 015 621.

Hunt, J. McV. (1961). *Intelligence and Experience*. New York: Ronald Press.

Majoribanks, K. (1979). Family Environments. In H.J. Walberg (Ed.), *Educational Environments and Effects*. Berkeley, CA: McCrutchan Publishing.

Siegel, D.F. (1990). The Literacy Press: A Process Model for Reading Development. *The Journal of Educational Research*, 83(6),336-347.

Siegel, D.F. & Hanson, R.A. (1992). Prescription for Literacy: Providing Critical Educational Experiences. *ERIC Digest*, D68, EDO-CS-92-01, Clearing House on Reading and Communication Skills, Indiana University.

Wolf, R.M. (1964). The Identification and Measurement of Environmental Process Variables Related to Intelligence. Unpublished doctoral dissertation, University of Chicago. See Figure 1 on beginning formal reading instruction

Notes

▼4▼

Learning School Reference Concepts in the Child's First Language:

A Guide for Parents as Teachers

By Huberto Molina

Introduction

Parents are a child's first and best teacher. In many cases, parents are not aware of how they can help their child. A parent may not be aware of the value of being a bilingual and may not know how to develop school-related skills in the first language to prepare one's child for success in the second language. A parent may even think that a first language interferes with second-language acquisition and ultimately with school success.

Those parents who recognize the value of the home language should be congratulated, for it is the avenue of communication between the child and those around him: mother, father, grandparents, other family members, and friends. These cultural links are very important from the standpoint of self-esteem. Additionally, such bilingual skills are related to cognitive development and add a valuable resource to the nation as it enlarges its global perspectives.

The purpose of this chapter is to acknowledge the importance of using a child's first language and to describe ways to use this asset in acquiring a second language. To put this discussion in concrete form, the child's first language is assumed to be Spanish; however, with modification, the strategies, approaches, and techniques described here apply to other first languages and dialects.

Transfer

Once concepts are learned in the first language, transfer of strategies and skills to the second language is an efficient and relatively easy task for the bilingual parent as teacher. Initially such strategies include very simple tasks such as pointing to items in the immediate environment, pointing to pictures, responses that require affirmative or negative indications, one-word responses, several-word responses, etc. Later, as a parent reads to the child, activities become more related to literacy, for example understanding the title of a story, left-to-right orientation, written words conveying meaning, spaces separating words, turning a page. All of these conventions can be learned in natural family settings.

Perhaps the most important concepts being acquired are the acknowledgment of the importance and the enjoyment associated with the experience of learning. All activities should be presented in the context of enjoyment and fun to encourage the transfer of positive feelings associated with the acquisition of new skills.

Methods

It is very important that the child receive such language-development experiences in a natural, non-stressful environment. This vocabulary presented below should be taught within a broad, natural approach which parents over the years have always provided. The five suggestions below will help parents introduce words and concepts to be presented informally:

1. The focus should be on meaning and comprehension with no attempt to focus on language or concept forms in isolation. The list provided is merely a guide, *e.g.*, in the context of *lejos* (far) you may want to use the word *cerca* (near) in a game or any informal setting.

2. Common everyday items should be used to make the concepts concrete, *e.g.*, use cups, plates, toys to teach the concept *tres*. In the same context review *una* tasa, *dos* tasas, *la tasa está sobre el plato, el plato está debajo de la tasa, el plato está al lado de la tasa*, etc.

3. In all language activities, the child should not be forced to speak, nor should an attempt be made to correct errors. All efforts should be rewarded in the caring manner that parents do so well.

4. Many of the words and concepts in the following guide may already exist in the vocabulary of a Spanish-speaking child. This makes success even more attainable. On the other hand, parents should not feel that the child must know every word and concept in this list; however, the more language and concepts the child knows coming to the school experience, the better. The list that follows may have to be adjusted to be consistent with the language used in the home, *e.g.*, the color *rojo* communicates equally as well as *colorado*.

5. Parents should use a variety of home language that is natural to them. Later on in school, bilingual teachers should accept and be acquainted with varieties of the child's home language and present the standard form to the child, thus adding to the student's linguistic repertoire. Here again, once a concept is learned, transfer to English is an easy task for the competent bilingual teacher.

Vocabulary List

The first vocabulary list is presented in Spanish, using twenty-three categories:

Palabras Y Conceptos de Comunicacion por Categorias

1. Objetos de la Escuela:

libro	creyón, crayola	silla
mesa	lápiz	pedazo de papel
bandera	cesto de basura	salón, clase
tapete	escuela	fila
escritorio	patio de recreo	biblioteca
pluma (de escribir)	cesto-, canasta	ilustración
tiza	pizarra, pizarrón	estante de libros

cuarto	niño (niños)	niña
maestra	gente	amigo, amiga
puerta	estante	

2. Actividades de la Escuela:

aprender	descansar, descansando	pintar, pintando
colorear (coloreando)	delgado, más delgado	el más delgado
vacío	lleno	mediado
mitad, medio	largo / corto	más largo, el más largo
más corto, el más corto	alto, pequeño	estrecho / ancho
igual	escribir, (escribiendo)	leer (leyendo)
cantar (cantando)	bailar (bailando)	enseñar (enseñando)
jugar (jugando)	dibujar (dibujando)	

3. Colores:

color	rojo, colorado	amarillo
azul	verde	negro
blanco	café	anaranjado
rosado	gris	morado

4. Descripción y Comparación:

diferente	igual	grande / pequeño
pesado, más pesado	liviano, más liviano	más grande, el más grande
el más pesado	el más liviano	el más ... que todos
callado / ruidoso	rápido	despacio
mínimo	más alto	más bajo
gordo	joven	viejo
más lento, el más lento	lentamente	encima / abajo
cerrado / abierto	sucio	limpio
mojado	seco	alto / bajo
muy, mucho	el más bajo	el más alto
bueno	muchísimo	nuevo
más viejo, el más viejo	correcto	incorrecto
más rápido, el más rápido	ruidosamente, con ruido	rápidamente
calladamente	más joven, el más joven	

5. Comida y Comiendo:

leche	jugo de naranja	café
agua	dulce, caramelo	limón
pan	carne	tomate(s)
vegetal, legumbre	huevo, blanquillo	fruta
pastel	helado, nieve	crecer (creciendo)
lechuga	taza	vaso
tazón, plato hondo	estufa	desayuno
cena, comida	almuerzo	tomar (tomando)
comer (comiendo)	comió	tomó
plato	manzana	plátano
naranja	cocinar (cocinando)	vajilla
cocina		

6. Matemáticas:

número	uno	dos
tres	cuatro	cinco
seis	siete	ocho

sumar, añadir	restar, menos	más
nueve	diez	once
doce	primero	último
segundo	tercer, tercero	cuarto
menos que	igual	contar (contando)
queda	curveado	línea, fila
derecho	círculo	cuadrado
triángulo	rectángulo	figura, forma
largo	ancho	

7. Ropa:

blusa	camisa	suéter
sombrero	abrigo	botón
zapato	calcetín, media	falda
impermeable	chaqueta	vestido
ropa	traje de baño	usar, vestir
usando, vistiendo	paraguas	

8. Aparatos:

periódico, papel	radio	televisor, televisión
revista	carta	hablar, conversación
teléfono		

9. Movimiento:

saltar (saltando)	atrapar (atrapando)	pegar
tirar, aventar	jalando, halando	empujando
romper (rompiendo)	roto	derramar (derramando)
columpiar (columpiando)	tomar (tomando)	tomó
mover	atrapó	tirado
caminar (caminando)	sentar (sentando)	traer
vino, llegó	cargar (cargando)	cerrar (cerrando)
venir (viniendo)	parar (parando)	tirar, dejar caer
ir (yendo)	fue	brincar (brincando)
saltar (saltando)	patear (pateando)	abrir
dar vuelta	hablar (hablando)	correr (corriendo)
corrió	vaciando, echando	apuntar (apuntando)

10. Partes del Cuerpo:

cabeza	boca	nariz
oreja	ojo(s)	dedo
mano	brazo	cuerpo
cara	pierna(s)	pies
pie		

11. Animales Domésticos:

gato	perro	caballo
pájaro	pez	gallina, pollo
vaca	animal, animales	tigre
pato		

12. Sentidos:

oir	escuchar	oler (oliendo)
querer	bien	enfermo
mirar	ver	sentir

feliz, contento	triste	amargo
dulce	hambre	cansado
probar	sediento	tocar (tocando)

13. Tiempo y Relaciones de Tiempo:

noche	reloj	hora, tiempo
calendario, almanaque	semana	lunes
domingo	martes	miércoles
jueves	viernes	mañana
sábado	hoy	oscuro
por (duración del tiempo)	hasta	temprano
tarde	cuando	día
esta noche	ayer	ahora
en punto		

14. Comunidad:

corral	finca, granja	zoológico
compró	compra, comprar	diez centavos
dinero	cinco centavos	centavo
edificio	tienda	cartero
doctor, médico	policía	bombero

15. Geografía:

loma	montaña	valle
océano, mar	río	ciudad
campo, país		

16. Música:

guitarra	piano	música
musical	instrumento	tambor

17. Recreación:

patines	nadar (nadando)	nadó
echando carreras	concha	pescando
beísbol, pelota	juguete(s)	playa
arena	películas	alberca, piscina
circo	viajar (viajando)	vacaciones
fútbol	deporte(s)	juego
perder	equipo	ganar (ganando)
perdió, perdido	carrera	parque, aparca, estacionar
ganó	nadó	pelota

18. Seguridad:

pare / siga	semáforo	banqueta, acera
fuego	herido	ayuda
autopista	esperar	duele
calle		

19. Hogar y Familia:

casa	familia	mamá
papá	botella	caja
sala de estar	sofá	lámpara
alfombra	ventana	árbol(es)
hermano	hermana	dormitorio, recámara

dormir (durmiendo)	peinar (peinando)	flor
zacate, césped	escalera	patio
jardín	madera	cama
plancha	hogar	pared
casa del perro	cerca	lavar (lavando)
jabón	toalla	cuarto de baño
garaje	visitar	limpiar
hombre	mujer, dama	

20. Transportación:

carro, auto	bicicleta	camión(es)
autobús	avión	tren
camino	barco	paseo, montar
paseando	paseó, montó	conducir, manejar
conduciendo, manejando	tractor	paseó, montó

21. Temperatura:

frío	caliente	tibio
con viento	nublado	otoño
primavera	verano	estación
nieve	invierno	llover, lloviendo
de lluvia	temperatura	

22. Conjuntos:

conjuntos	par(es)	unos de
piezas	juntos	todos
partes de		

23. Relaciones de Espacio:

enfrente de	atrás de	lejos
cerca	detrás	sobre, encima, en
al lado	debajo, abajo	entre
después	arriba	izquierda
derecha	por	adentro
encima de	al cruzar	alrededor
antes	afuera	hacia
lejos	allá, allí	afuera. fuera de
adentro, dentro, en	a través	aquí

Multilingual/Multicultural Application

The list that follows is in English, presenting the similar terms in similar categories, and can be used as a guide in developing vocabulary and concept versions in other languages

Words and Concepts by Communication Category

1. School Objects:

book	crayon	chair
table	pencil	piece of paper
flag	wastebasket	classroom
mat	school	row
desk	playground	library

pen	basket	picture
chalk	blackboard	bookshelf
room	boy	girl
children	teacher	people
friend	door	shelf

2. School Activities:

learn	rest(ing)	paint(ing)
color(ing)	write(ing)	read(ing)
sing(ing)	dance(ing)	teach(ing)
play(ing)	draw(ing)	

3. Colors:

color (noun)	red	yellow
blue	green	black
white	brown	orange
pink	gray	purple

4. Description and Comparison:

not the same	same	big/little
heavy	light	heavier
lighter	bigger	biggest
heaviest	lightest	most
thin	thinner	thinnest
empty	full	half-full
half	long / short	longer
longest	shorter	shortest
tall / small	narrow / wide	alike
dirty	clean	wet
dry	high / low	very
lowest	different	highest
good	very much	new
old	older	oldest
right	wrong	taller
tallest	faster	fastest
noisily	quickly	quietly
younger	youngest	closed / open
top / bottom	quiet / noisy	quick
slow	least	higher / lower
fat	young	old
slower / slowest	slowly	

5. Mathematics:

number	one	two
three	four	five
six	seven	eight
nine	ten	eleven
twelve	first	last
second	third	fourth
fewer	more	equal
unequal	take away	count
left	curved	line
straight	circle	square
triangle	rectangle	shape

length	width	

6. Sets:

set	pair	ones
piece	together	all
part		

7. Space Relations:

in front	in back	far
near	behind	above
beside	below	between
under	after	down
up	left	right
by	inside	next to
across	around	before
outside	toward	away
there	out	in
through	here	

8. Clothing:

blouse	shirt	sweater
hat	coat	button
shoe(s)	sock(s)	skirt
raincoat	jacket	dress
clothes	bathing suit	wear(ing)
umbrella		

9. Food and Eating:

apple	banana	orange
milk	orange juice	coffee
water	candy	lemon
bread	meat	tomato(es)
vegetable	egg	fruit
cake	ice cream	pie
grow(ing)	lettuce	cup
glass	bowl	stove
breakfast .	dinner	lunch
drink(ing)	eat(ing)	ate
drank	plate	cook(ing)
dishes	kitchen	

10. Home and Family:

house	family	mama
papa	bottle	box
living room	couch	lamp
rug	window	tree(s)
brother	sister	bedroom
sleep(ing)	comb(ing)	flower
glass	ladder	backyard
garden	wood	bed
iron	home	wall
doghouse	fence	wash(ing)
soap	towel	bathroom
garage	visit	clean(verb)

| man | woman | lady |

11. Devices:

newspaper	radio	T.V.
magazine	letter	talk
telephone	television	

12. Movement:

jump(ing)	catch(ing)	hit
throw(ing)	pulling	pushing
break(ing)	broke	spill(ing)
back and forth	swing(ing)	take(ing)
took	move	caught
thrown	walk(ing)	sit(ting)
bring	came	carry(ing)
close(ing)	come(ing)	stand(ing)
drop	go(ing)	went
hop(ping)	jump(ing)	kick(ing)
open	turn	talk(ing)
run(ning)	ran	pouring
point(ing)		

13. Parts of the Body:

head	mouth	nose
ear	eye(s)	finger
hand	arm(s)	body
face	leg(s)	feet
foot		

14. Pets:

cat	dog	horse
bird	fish	chicken
cow	animal(s)	tiger
duck		

15. Senses:

hear	listen	smell
want	fine	sick
look	see	feel
happy	sad	sour
sweet	hungry	tired
taste	thirsty	touch(ing)
watch		

16. Time and Temporal Relations:

night	clock	time
calendar	week	Sunday
Monday	Tuesday	Wednesday
Thursday	Friday	Saturday
morning	today	tomorrow
dark	for (duration of time)	until
early	late	when
day	tonight	yesterday
afternoon	now	o'clock

17. Community:

farmyard	farm	zoo
bought	buy	dime
money	nickel	penny
building	store	mailman
doctor	policeman	fireman

18. Geography:

hill	mountain(s)	valley
ocean	river	city
country		

19. Music:

guitar	piano	music
musical	instrument	drum

20. Recreation:

skates	swim(ming)	swam
racing	shell	fishing
baseball	toy(s)	beach
sand	movies	swimming pool
circus	travel(ling)	vacation
football	sport(s)	game
lose	team	win(ning)
lost	race(ing)	park
won	ball	

21. Safety:

stop / go	traffic light	sidewalk
fire	hurt	help
freeway	wait	hurts
street		

22. Transportation:

car	bike	truck(s)
bus	airplane	train
road	boat	ride
riding	rode	drive
driving	drove	tractor
rode	plane	

23. Weather:

cold	hot	warm
windy	cloudy	rain (verb)
fall	spring	summer
season	snow	winter
rain(ing)	rainy	weather

Reference

Molina, Huberto. *English Language and Concepts Program for Spanish-Speaking Children: Technical Specifications*. Los Alamitos, CA: SWRL Educational Research and Development, Undated.

Instructional Decisions Based on Second-Language and Socio-Cultural Research

By Huberto Molina

Components Which Play a Major Role in Instructional Decisions: Theory, Research, School Context

This chapter is concerned with relating second-language acquisition and socio-cultural research findings to instructional decision making. In order for strategies and methods to be effective, attention has to be directed to underlying components which play a major role in the decisions:

1. Second-language acquisition theories which underlie such decisions.

2. Research findings which support instructional treatments and point to other equally relevant areas, *e.g.*, socio-cultural concerns.

3. The above must be considered in the context of the classroom experience as we relate these considerations to instruction.

There is debate over which is the best second-language theory; however, there is agreement about some basic ideas concerning how the language skills are acquired and in what contexts:

1. Comprehensible input in low-anxiety environment is considered essential in the process.

2. Negotiation of meaning plays a key role.

3. Meaningful communication involves several developmental levels in terms of what the learner can do now and what the learner can do in the future. Progress through these levels occurs by meaningful communication.

4. Connections from the student's experience add reality, and relevance, providing meaning to classroom instruction.

Research in the area of socio-cultural contexts extends the concern for providing educational opportunity to the second-language learner beyond the domain of literacy into other areas such as the following:

1. Equity:
   ◆ Some minority members operate in a perceived caste-like system.
   ◆ Equity in the classroom

2. Joining the work force in society.

3. Fostering effective understanding, personal relations between students.

4. Cultural experiences in the classroom that demonstrate how cultures differ, yet have a great deal in common.

5. How do we encourage minority members to become educators?

6. What is the teacher role in regard to drop-out rates?

7. What can teachers do to provide students with an analytic view in regard to the media?

Another important input to instruction is the school context which includes:

1. The demographics describing the student population.

2. The financial resources of the community.

3. The local, state, and national political environment.

4. The availability of bilingual teachers.

5. The general attitude toward members of the minority language group.

The interaction of theory, research, and school context result in decision making that has direct influence on classroom instruction. Such interaction is illustrated below:

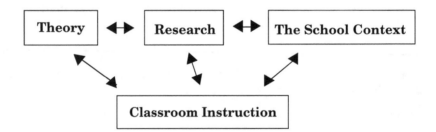

Theory, research, and school context as described in the above discussion extend far beyond the domain of the classroom. However, it is in the classroom where instruction takes place. The teacher has the opportunity to provide meaningful input during the instructional period that the outside world may not be able to do. The teacher also creates a classroom culture that promotes attitudes and critical-thinking skills by which students can critically interpret the sociocultural framework in which they live.

Approaches and Methods in Use in the Classroom

There is a great deal of research in the field supporting the following approaches and methods that are currently in use in many classrooms:

1. Cooperative Learning.

2. Sheltered English/SDAIE.

3. Thematic Teaching.

4. Tutorials.

5. Total Physical Response (TPR).

6. Culture.

7. Second-language teaching skills.

8. Classroom management:
   ◆ Lesson plan format.
   ◆ Presentation.
   ◆ Equity considerations.

9. Assessment.

Classroom Supports

The classroom can typically provide the following instructional supports:

1. Bulletin boards, walls, ceilings, windows, floor, doors.

2. Flannel boards.

3. Picture files.

4. Learning centers.

5. Closely-related resources: parental support, school sponsored workshops, public libraries, daily newspapers.

Computers are also being used in a growing number of schools, and many rapidly-expanding applications are making their presence known in classrooms.

Making Instructional Decisions

The primary question to be addressed is: What classroom strategy do we employ to effectively utilize theory, research, instructional approaches, and readily-available classroom supports.

To help address this challenge, a format entitled "Instructional Decisions Based on Research Findings" is presented on the followin page. The format includes the following information:

1. Problem identified by researcher.

2. Instructional goal or objective.

3. Relevant approaches and supports available to the classroom.

The Format:
"Instructional Decisions Based on Research Findings"

Problem Identified by Researchers:

_____

_____

_____

Researcher(s):

_____

Instructional Goal or Objective:

_____

_____

_____

Approaches and Methods:

    1. Cooperative Learning.

    2. Sheltered English/Specially Designed Academic Instruction in English (S.D.A.I.E).

    3. Thematic Approach.

    4. Tutorials (Peer, Parent, Teacher Assistant).

    5. Total Physical Response.

    6. Culture.

Relevant Classroom Supports:

    7. Bulletin boards, walls, ceilings, windows, floor.

    8. Flannel board.

    9. Picture files.

    10. Learning centers.

    11. Daily newspapers.

    12. Parent participation.

    13. Classroom Management:
        • Lesson format.
        • Lesson presentation.
        • Equity.

    14. Computer in the classroom.

    15. Assessment.

The Format in Operation (Sample 1):
Counteracting Student Perceptions of Caste-Like Role

To illustrate the use of the proposed format, a research problem originally identified by John Ogbu is presented. The researcher states that some minority members due to bias and discrimination accept a role that does not allow them to act as Americans with opportunities that mainstream members enjoy. Thus, they operate within a perceived caste-like system. Following, approaches and classroom supports are described in reference to the goal or objective. Additional use of approaches and supports will undoubtedly be incorporated by the creative teacher.

"Instructional Decisions Based on Research Findings"

Problem Identified by Researcher:

Due to bias and discrimination some minorities members accept a role that does not allow them to act as Americans with opportunities that mainstream members enjoy. Thus, they operate within a perceived caste-like system.

Researcher:

John U. Ogbu.

Instructional Goal or Objective:

Present learning experiences to counteract perceptions of expected caste-like behavior and provide opportunity for school success.

Approaches and Methods:

1. Cooperative Learning: Form groups into homogeneous and heterogeneous groups so that social interaction between racial groups is encouraged. This method is also used in Sheltered English/SDAIE as described below.

2. Sheltered English/Specially Designed Academic Instruction in English (S.D.A.I.E): For speakers of another language learning English this approach is very important in regard to joining mainstream instruction.

This approach in teaching of K-12 grade level subject matter in English is most appropriate for students who already have achieved basic literacy skills in the first language and have demonstrated a basic proficiency in English and are now ready to acquire cognitive, academic language proficiency. Because of these two prerequisites, a great deal of care must be given to instruction in the first language and initial instruction in English to ensure that students master an appropriate threshold of the first language and an appropriate level of basic English. The techniques described below apply equally as well to instruction in the first language and early second-language instruction when basic English skills are being acquired.

The third and fourth grades are specially difficult for limited-English speakers, for normally this is the beginning of more abstract, cognitively demanding instruction. It is at this time that Sheltered English/SDAIE is most valuable. It is very important for these students to receive Sheltered English/SDAIE instruction at this time to acquire prerequisite skills as efficiently as possible, for mainstream students are progressing in their classes too. Playing "catch-up" is an especially difficult process in the core curriculum. Sheltered English/SDAIE can provide essential skills to empower limited-English speakers to have an equitable entry into the core curriculum.

Procedures for the teacher to assure comprehensible input for all students:

+ All students should be able to hear and see the teacher.

+ Clear articulation.

◆ Rate of speech-slow enough to be understood but yet maintain authentic intonation.

◆ Use high-frequency words.

◆ Use short sentences.

◆ Use real objects, pictures, and manipulatives.

◆ Act out, role play, use puppets.

◆ Explain using different words, thus adding to what students already know.

◆ Encourage use of questions.

◆ Allow students time to react.

◆ Model non-linguistic ways of communication by using gestures.

◆ Use Total Physical Response (TPR) procedures in the beginning of language acquisition process. Also use it to check comprehension and for variety throughout the language acquisition process.

◆ Keep meaning as a high priority item as you present oral and written language instruction.

◆ Connect classroom instruction to the student's experience and home background.

◆ Relate previous experience to new experience by outlining, by using thematic teaching.

◆ Rather than correcting directly, model good language usage.

◆ Include higher-level thinking tasks, *e.g.*, in classification tasks discuss criteria used for the basis of the classification.

◆ Use Bloom's Taxonomy as well as techniques such as brainstorming, predicting outcomes, comparing/contrasting, defending.

◆ Teach "how to learn" skills, *e.g.*, note-taking, outlining, summarizing, using the library, time management.

◆ Subject matter content:
   Identify key topics and organize around main themes.
   Identify concepts and relate to "hands-on" materials
   Make objectives and instruction explicit.
   Incorporate assessment as a daily and follow-up process.

In those situations where bilingual education is not provided, *e.g.*, the English-Language Development Program (ELP), a much more difficult instructional problem exists, for English-language learners do not have a conceptual knowledge base that they can use to transfer previously learned first-language skills. In whatever program these students are instructed, it is important that the suggested Sheltered English/SDAIE techniques and follow-up assessment procedures be used to ensure that limited-English-speakers have educational opportunity to succeed in mainstream classes.

3. Thematic Approach: Stress appropriate academic attitudes and reward perseverance. Relate existing academic skills to new skills.

4. Tutorial (Peer, Parent, Assistant): Provide training opportunities to assure equitable opportunity for all students.

5. Total Physical Response: Use TPR at various places throughout the program to ensure that conceptual information is meaningful to students.

6 . Culture: Foster respect for all cultures. Refer to discussion on this subject in the chapter "Ways to Empower the Second Language Classroom" in this text.

Classroom Supports:

7. Bulletin boards, walls, ceiling, windows, floor: Promote pride and ownership in the classroom by extensively displaying student work. Displays can demonstrate the improvement in the skill process.

8. Flannel boards: Use to promote verbal interaction. Use small boards for cooperative learning experiences.

9. Picture files: Use pictures that portray the diversity of people in our country in a variety of roles to dispel stereotypes.

10. Learning centers: Present career opportunities within our society. Relate the relevancy of skills being acquired to careers.

11. Daily newspapers: Use the newspaper to relate career goals by reading to students or by making reading assignments. Develop student ability to identify fact from opinion by analyzing newspaper stories.

12. Parent participation (home, school): Invite parent participation in the instructional process. Use the background and experiences of parents as a positive, rich resource.

13. Classroom management:

- ◆ Lesson Format: Structure into segments that make success available.

- ◆ Model expected classroom behaviors by role-playing.

- ◆ Lesson Presentation: Refer to chapter I, the Teacher and Comprehensible Input.

- ◆ Equity: Give attention, reward and praise students equally. In regard to paraprofessionals go over lesson content with aides and monitor student progress to assure equal access to core curriculum to all students in your classrooms.

14. Computer in the Classroom: Include this technology and emphasize its present and future potential value in students' careers. Use the computer as an incentive device by making students aware that literacy skills make it possible to communicate through the computer, *e.g.*, on-line.

15. Assessment: Reward perseverance: Include both group and individual accountability .

After limited-English students join mainstream, core instruction, follow up their progress to ensure that Sheltered/English/SDAIE has provided the necessary preparation. See the section "Ways to Empower the Second Language Classroom" in which assessing effectiveness is described under the title "Language and Content Items in Sheltered English".

The Format in Operation (Sample 2):
Error Correction Without Negative Effects

Another sample use of the format follows. This one is related to second-language acquisition. The problem considered here concerns error correction and the recognition of the need for low anxiety in the language-acquisition process.

Does this mean that there is no room in the classroom for error correction besides modeling correct responses? The following format makes explicit where error correction can take place.

"Instructional Decisions Based on Research Findings"

Problem Identified by Researcher:
Stephen Krashen and others have described the negative effects of error correction in teacher-presented lessons.

Researcher:
Stephen Krashen.

Instructional Goal or Objective:
Present error correction in the classroom where it does not interfere with the acquisition process.

Approaches and Methods:

1. Cooperative Learning: Train students in modeling techniques.

2. Sheltered English/Specially Designed Academic Instruction in English (S.D.A.I.E).

3. Thematic Approach: Relate acquired concepts and vocabulary across subject-matter disciplines to provide comprehensible input.

4. Tutorial (Peer. Parent, Assistant): Train tutors in modeling techniques.

5. Total Physical Response: Use where needed to ensure meaning in all levels of instruction.

6. Culture: Stress pride and respect for all cultures.

Classroom Support:

7. Bulletin boards, walls, ceiling, windows, floor: Provide opportunity for self-correction.

8. Flannel boards: Use flannel boards to provide comprehensible input and for verification of form in the writing process.

9. Picture files: Use where needed to ensure meaning.

10. Learning centers: Use extensively to provide practice. Self-correcting devices can be a part of the design requirement of learning centers. Thus students can engage in re-enforcing language-related activities without teacher supervision and control. This type of activity lends itself well to practice in many lessons in which students can compare their responses to those provided on an answer sheet. By following the design requirements of the learning center format, these activities can be fun and provide a low anxiety, pleasurable learning experience.

11. Daily newspapers: Use newspaper articles as a self-correction device. Students compare a dictated story to the actual newspaper article. This adds reality to punctuation, spelling, and literacy skills

12. Parent participation (home, school): Train parents in modeling techniques.

13. Classroom management (lesson format, lesson presentation, equity): Model correct responses when needed.

14. Computers in the classroom: Use programs with built-in self correction.

15. Assessment: Use assessment as a diagnostic tool to provide instruction where needed.

The Format in Operation (Sample 3): Language Acquisition

Following is an another example of the use the format in the context of language acquisition. Related to the previous problem which concerned error correction, this sample format is concerned with independent paper and pencil practice, *e.g.*, punctuation, matching shapes, identifying geographical locations, etc. While these appropriate practice activities can he tedious in a teacher-directed lesson, activities can be presented in the learning center format that can be fun.

"Instructional Decisions Based on Research Findings"

Problem Identified by Researcher:
Teacher-presented drills interfere with the aims of language acquisition.

Researchers:
Stephen Krashen and Tracy Terrell.

Instructional Goal or Objective:
Present language-reinforcing activities in a context where they do not interfere with language fluency.

Approaches and Methods:

1. Cooperative Learning: Prepare interactive activities which put to practice skills acquired in the classroom.

2. Sheltered English/Specially Designed Academic Instruction in English (S.D.A.I.E): Use techniques that make academic instruction comprehensible, avoiding drills.

3. Thematic Approach: Relate subject-matter content with the language-acquisition process, relating various areas, *e.g.*, math/science/social studies, avoiding teacher presented drills.

4. Tutorial (Peer, Parent, Assistant): Train tutors in SDAI techniques.

5. Total Physical Response: Use where needed by using objects, picture files, etc.

6. Culture: Incorporate artifacts, illustrations to acknowledge contributions made by world cultures. These hands-on materials support language acquisition without drills.

Classroom Support:

7. Bulletin boards, walls, ceiling, windows, floor: Use these in learning activities in which students can point to objects, punctuate, match shapes at their own speed, *e.g.*, students match names of countries to countries depicted on a map, punctuate a sentence, and then compare it to the answer sheets.

8. Flannel boards: Use flannel boards to practice both language-acquired and subject-matter content.

9. Picture files: Use to stimulate oral and written work.

10. Learning centers: Use learning centers to practice and reinforce skills learned in class. Work sheets can be used in the context of the design of learning centers.

11. Daily newspapers: Use newspapers as a tool to make reading and writing a realistic activity.

12. Parent participation (home, school): Send student-generated work home so that parents can be aware of school process, *e.g.*, a story written by the child.

13. Classroom management (lesson forma, lesson presentation, equity): Keep a focus on language acquisition in teacher presentations. Design attractive bulletin boards and learning centers to practice the acquired language and concept skills.

14. Computers in the classroom: Use programs which review and supplement the teacher presentation.

15. Assessment: Assess students consistency with classroom goals and objectives which include thinking skills that go beyond just memory.

References

Krashen, S, & Terrell, T.D. (1983). *The Natural Approach*. Oxford, United Kingdom: Pergamon Press.
Ogbu, J. (1995). Understanding Cultural Diversity and Learning. *Handbook of Research on Multicultural Education*. New York: Macmillan.

Other Books
from Caddo Gap Press
▼ ▼

The MESA Way: A Success Story of Nurturing Minorities for Math/Science-Based Careers by Wilbur H. Somerton, Mary Perry Smith, Robert Finnell & Ted W. Fuller, 1994, 212 pp., paper, $17.95, ISBN 1-880192-10-1.

The story of the MESA Program, started at the University of California, Berkeley, and replicated across California and the United States during the past two decades, stressing cooperation between universities, public schools, communities, and industry, all leading to significant student success.

National Association for Multicultural Education 1993 & 1994 Proceedings edited by Carl A. Grant, 1995, 454 pp., paper, $24.95.

Assembled papers and presentations from the 1993 and 1994 conferences of the National Association for Multicultural Education, offering the latest in theory and practice in the field.

Seeking Effective Schools for African American Children by Bunyan Bryant & Alan H. Jones, 1993, 80 pp., paper, $11.95, ISBN 1-880192-01-2.

An examination of the problems facing minority-population schools with solutions based on the effective schools principles developed by Ronald Edmunds.

Transforming the Curriculum for Multicultural Understandings: A Practitioner's Handbook by James B. Boyer & H. Prentice Baptiste, Jr., 1996, 266 pp., paper, $19.95, ISBN 1-880192-19-5.

Straight-forward and practical guidance for educators seeking to bring multicultural understadings and practices to their teaching, classrooms, schools, and communities.

Yesterday, Today & Tomorrow: Meeting the Challenge of Our Multicultural America & Beyond by Paul D. Christiansen & Michelle Young, 1996, 376 pp., paper, $29.95, ISBN 1-880192-18-7.

This unuual and exciting volume paints the panorama of diversity that is the United States through the presentation of numerous personal stories of individuals coming to America from a wide variety of ethnic, racial, national, and religious backgrounds, all woven into a moving narrative that highlights the evils of prejudice and discrimination and offers suggestions for understanding and celebrating diversity.

All of these books are available from
Caddo Gap Press, 3145 Geary Boulevard, Suite 275, San Francisco, Califdornia 94118, U.S.A.
e-mail caddogap@aol.com

Additional copies of

Empowering the Second-Language Classroom

**are availble from
Caddo Gap Press**

To order, use the form below:

Please send me _____ copies of ***Empowering the Second-Language Classroom*** at $19.95 each (plus shipping costs of $2 for the first book and $1 for each additional copy).

Name _____

Address _____

City, State & ZIPcode _____

❏ Check enclosed payable to Caddo Gap Press.

❏ Purchase order attached.

❏ Please charge my credit card:
    ❏ Visa or ❏ MasterCard

    Card Number _____ Expiration Date _____

    Signature _____

Mail completed form with payment to:
Caddo Gap Press
3145 Geary Boulevard, Suite 275
San Francisco, California 94118, U.S.A.